PENIS ENVY

101 THINGS TO DO IF YOU THINK YOUR PENIS IS TOO SMALL

by

RICKY BLEDSOE

edited by

LAURIE LAMSON

Edited by Laurie Lamson
Cover design by Jasmine D. Wilson
Cover illustration by Devin Martin and Jasmine D. Wilson

Printed in the U.S.A.

ISBN 0-982-63050-6

info and discussion forum available at:
www.mypenisenvy.com

dedicated to guys like me

A Note From The Editor

Penis Envy: 101 Things To Do If You Think Your Penis Is Too Small offers humorous insight and practical advice for penis-insecure men who obsess over the question: *does size really matter?*

Nothing is held back in this man-to-man self-help book, packed with valuable tips for guys who want richer, more enjoyable lives, regardless of penis size.

The book was conceived and written by Ricky Bledsoe after he heard Whoopie Goldberg on The Oprah Winfrey Show announce, *"What makes a good book is a subject you're passionate or obsessed about"*. Whoopie's statement got him thinking… the emotional and practical difficulty of living with penis envy was a subject Ricky was somewhat obsessed about.

Though guys are understandably reluctant to talk about it, he had hundreds of conversations, and found men from all walks of life would passionately participate in the discussion – once he introduced the topic. He also found that many were torturing themselves over it, just like he did.

A man who learned to make the best of his own 'predicament', Ricky hopes the book will also help female readers gain more understanding of how men think.

TABLE OF CONTENTS

PART X: YOU'RE MORE THAN JUST A SMALL PENIS!

PREFACE

QUESTION...

What do you think is the worst thing you could do to someone? Okay, well, maybe not the worst, but how 'bout in the top five?... Hmmm, let's see...

There's murder, of course, robbing them of their life. Then there's stealing from them – whether a car, wife or life savings. Or physically hurting them to the point of hospitalization. Yeah, those are typical, easily rolling outta someone's thoughts.

But how about something more effective, like torture?

Torture has got to be one of the worst things you could do to someone, physically and mentally. And in some folklore, torture is worse than death. The various degrees of continuous physical sharp pains inflicted are devastating to the body. Although, undergoing it seems an eternity, usually the whole ordeal is over quickly.

Mental torture, however, is incomparable, unlike anything else, and often personal and invasive. And oh yeah, I forgot... the time factor is indefinite, and often lingers throughout life...

When it's between man and woman, public and private humiliation are also along those lines of the worst thing you could do to someone. If it's that bad, it usually starts off private. Then some scorned bitch, who wasn't pretty enough in the first place, decides to air his private business and his shortcomings just because after a brief sexual relation he didn't want to have anything to do with her anymore! Uhh, did we kinda get off the *question*?

POINTS TO PONDER...

People are largely made up of their past and experiences. But more powerful than the actual experience itself are the words expressed during the experience. Or words not expressed at all, but facial gestures and body language with implied meaning. It is a shame how an immature adolescent boy's mind can be affected and influenced by a maturing adolescent girl who just so happened to have had more dick than a young rising porno star in the last year. It would seem that a young girl instinctively knows she matures much faster than any young boy ever could, but also realizes her reign is swift and short-lived, and that she will soon be reigned over... As she approaches her later teens she experiences her control slipping away. She needs a quick way to cut a man down like a tree. She could revert back to her old ways with a swift kick to the balls, but the effects were too temporal. Since she is naturally physically weaker, she needed an alternate control; a trump card of hurtful words that could cut to the bone, perhaps.

She knew that dick subdued her, but made him strong and cocky. But just a few words of ridicule from her about his dick instantly took his self-esteem and challenged his manhood. She seen this as an *Ace in the Hole* that she could readily use on most men in time of desperate need. So, early womanhood allowed her to devise her very own crash course: *'Man Manipulation 101'*... She passed with flying colors. (I thought you knew).

I wrote this book because of the continuous mental ill feeling I had about my penis size and my sexual performance. I was obsessed about these shortcomings for years (no pun intended). The only thing that kept me afloat was getting a girl who looked decent enough to walk around with and didn't seem to care about what I thought were my embarrassments. But even if she did treat me like a king, my manhood was already scarred for life early on because of a few loose pussy sluts who passed-that-ass around like a joint of reefer amongst rebellious junior high students.

EPISODE 1...

My first terrible experience was, I believe, in the 9th grade.

Her name was Adrianne. She had the body of an African ghetto queen. I mean that ass was huge! But had a ridiculously beautiful shape to it. Her skin tone dark as the blackest African, but smooth as silk. And her hair looked like she came from a tribal colony in Africa because it was nappy as fuck! And only *that* long. (And yes, I did snap my fingers when I said, *that* long). Anyway, I couldn't see the 'forest for the trees' because she liked me and I liked that ass she was wearing. I mean that ass was scrump-deli-o-cious looking. And even though I knew I didn't have enough dick for the task, I wanted to penetrate that ass anyway – just like all the rest of the sexual loser junior high school students. But she wanted to give that pussy to little dick Rick. (But like my uncle always said, "I shouldda known betta, icky dicky baby, aww shuxx"... Kennythurl, Maxeray? *Inside joke fellahs, pay no attention.*)

Anyway, my dick was hard from the time we talked during P.E. class, until school was out; from the bus ride home with her, to my father's bedroom (I *had* to use the king size bed, of course). Believe me, I was ready to bust-a-load way back in P.E. class when she said "yes", with those tight gym shorts on!

Then, when she took off her clothes and displayed her big ass with full hips to back it up, my dumb ass committed my first 'combination bust-a-load rookie mistake'... I put my hand on that ass! What an *idiot* move! I laid her down, slipped my dick in her pussy, stroked that drenched wet sloppy mess about 3 times and released the floodgates with great fury! Then the big pussy-whore had the nerve to ask me, "Why did you cum so quick?"

Well fellahs, let me tell ya, it wasn't because of her volcano-wet canyon-size pussy, because she was so black I never really seen it. And her pussy was so fuckin' big I barely felt any walls. Felt like someone had just opened the front door for me to walk in and I accidentally brushed across the door-jam with way too much vaseline on it. Anyway, I think it was her fault. The punk-whore shouldn't have made me sit next to her big-hipped-ass on the bus ride home with her trigger-finger fuckin'

with my loaded gun! What a 'prostitute' move, that was, fuckin'
cunt! Bitch must've been undercover, 'cause only 20-year vets
do shit like that; keep fuckin' with your dick trying to make you
cum quick so they can get-the-money-and-step before you even
get the pussy good.

Needless to say, after that 'let off', I couldn't get my dick hard,
even after 40 minutes. Then, the slippery-snatch skank had the
nerve to say, *"Maybe sex isn't for you..."* Fellahs, let me tell
you, I was shocked, speechless, hard-dickless, and devastated!
That whole ordeal fucked my mind up way into adulthood.
From that point on, I believed my penis was too small *and* I
didn't have any dick control.

EPISODE 2...

This next "hooker" episode was with a bitch in high school. A
straight fucking car-hop! Black-Indian mixed looking girl who
ran track with gorgeous legs and a bomb-shaped ass to go with
it. I think her name was Nina... At this time I was a sorta bow-
legged kid playing baseball. This car-hop hoe was originally
infatuated with my brother - or was it his car...I don't know.
But my brother was good-looking, had plenty of pretty girls,
and plenty of top-of-the-line cars; Turbo Porsche, Benz, and
plenty street-race fixers in the early 80's. At this time, I hadn't
got my first car yet. And nympho Nina wouldn't lay eyes on
me, let alone say two words to me. She kept hanging around
my brother's house and that fuckin' car.

Thing is, I don't even think my brother ever took her serious.
After all, he always had "dimes" to choose from, and she was
probably just a low-budget 8. After a short while she learned
Robby was my brother and allowed him to introduce her to me.
Couldn't have been more than 5 seconds later this car-hop bitch
was gettin' in the passenger seat jammin' the Alpine system
with all the lime green lights and the thin detached EQ on the
bottom with the line-lights spreading across with the beat.

All I know is that I wanted to fuck this bitch just as bad as she
wanted to ride in that souped-up Celica. Well, maybe not *that*

bad! After a while, my brother was ready to sell the Celica, and gave me first dibs on buying it. I told him it was too much money and couldn't afford to buy it. Then he mentioned the name *"Nina"*, and somehow, miraculously, I came up with the money! All of it! Let me tell ya, that carhop hoe's eyes rolled straight off my brother and stared dead at me! I believe that day was the first time I actually noticed the color of her eyes were brown...probably because she was so-full-of-shit! (I know, that line was not *that* original.). That bitch was too young & dumb for him, anyway. Here he was graduating to a Porsche, and I was getting a used Toyota. What a stupid slut. Now, I was the talk of the school, and nympho Nina was lookin' at me. In no time flat, I had her back at my house. Only this time, I chose my own bed (twin-size, that is), I mean, fuck that, *I* had the bad-ass car, not this hooker!

She took off her clothes and was incredibly smooth, unbelievable. Then I took off my clothes and smiled at her. There we stood both naked. She looked at me up & down, and, with sorta contempt said, *"I thought you had a big-ass dick! – 'cause you was all bow-legged"*...

Gentleman, let me tell ya, those were hurtful words, true enough. But the ill effects were watered-down due to the fact she was checkin' me out at school for some time and I didn't even know it! However, the girl went with her *sick* frame-of-mind and ruled her judgment on the car and not on me... so she fucked me anyway...

Truth is, this nympho rode my dick like a bull-riding cowgirl and damn near broke it. She let me hit it from all angles. She didn't make hardly any noise like I had hoped, but I did feel her pussy walls all around, so I was sorta pleased at that. Not to mention I lasted way longer than 3 minutes. Of course, I still believed my penis was too small. I came too fast and don't believe she came at all...

To my dismay, I never got that pussy again... And I don't believe she was ever interested in my car anymore. But now I look back on it and think, 'Hey, I didn't do that bad. I felt all pussy walls... Ain't my fault she got her pussy beat-up to no sensation by car-hopping dick-to-dick around town.'

INTERMISSION...

By the 12th grade, things were changing for the better in the way of girls, and my sexual performances. All of a sudden, I was having a couple of girlfriends that were totally sexually compatible with me, my size, and my performance. For sure, my dick didn't get any bigger. I just ended up meeting girls who were damn near perfect for me. Girls whom I was dominating in bed. And girls who I was running outta bed. And I also met girls who were jumpin' up & down, screaming & hollering out my name during sex...sayin' shit like, *"Aw! you small di-... I Mean, big dick motherfucker! Take that Vienna Sausage.... I mean, Big Hillshire Farm Sausage outta my pussy! You're ticklin... I mean, killing me!"* You know, all those bald-faced lies these professional hookers tell you.

EPISODE 3...

But shortly after high school, I ended up going to jail. And getting tossed in the dungeon along with hundreds of other inmates, whose crimes spanned from murder, kidnap, rape, to petty theft. In tha Big House, man, doin' time and housed with guys from just about every cultural society. From Vietnamese gangs who rob their own neighbors of their life savings kept in the home - preying on their elderly fear of dealing with commercial banks. To hot-headed Mexicans' temporary misguided comraderie, too jealous over their women, and too macho to let-it-go...another murder rap. To Blacks, no comraderie, impatient, envious, and too much hate for self. In jail for the silliest crimes and getting the most time. To Whites, the deepest in mental disturbance. Repeating sick crimes of rape, murder, and child molestation; yet also the most unpredictable, cunning, and the cleverest of the minds. Constantly succeeding at swindling the federal government and big business. His efforts have earned him the title of the most dangerous of inmates. And for some sad revengeful reason, the guys love to see another White brought down, in hopes his crimes live up to the stereotype; sick and deranged. If so, boring monotony can be replaced by instigative gossip insuring perverse violence within the White race - an awaited sight to see... Now, just what do these racial criminal profiles have to do with big dicks and little dick complexes? Absolutely nothing... I just thought I should tell you what I noticed while I was in there.

EPISODE 4...

But what really threw-me-for-a-loop was the strong presence of openly gay males and she-males alike - men whom I always thought to have penis envy at an early age. And men whom I felt the most uneasy around. Not because more than not they seemed to be interested in me, but the fact that they have in-your-face penis envy. You know, you catch them staring at your face until you both make eye contact, then, in that very 2-second moment you catch them 3-times looking down at your crotch area, then slowly rolling their eyes back up to yours, only to notice their even more seductive looks.

One she-male episode I'll never forget took place when I first got in the slammer. She, I mean 'he' kept trying to get my attention as the guard walked me through the cellblock to locate my cell. When I did look back the she-male kept twisting around showing me his ass. Now mind you, he was fully dressed like the rest of the inmates, but wearing pants a few sizes smaller, of course. He was Black, and his face looked like an ugly girl. But to my amazement, he had a big ass that was shaped just like a woman's. Later that day, it was time to take showers. About 15 to 20 inmates had to shower together in one big open shower area. When my group lined up for next-in, his group was already showering. I could see her, I mean him. He was looking at me, and was already turned around with that big ass showing. But then something startled me. And quite scared the shit out of me. He turned around for his frontal area to face me. I couldn't believe what I saw... This Dude had a dick as thick as a coke can! - and hung down damn near to his knee! I must say, he caught me for a few seconds like a deer in headlights. He even started to get a little aroused. Then, shower rotation was ordered. I didn't see him til later that day when phone call opportunity was announced. He spotted me across the room and said rather loudly, *"I seen you lookin' at ma ass in the shower. You can't stop thinkin' 'bout this big juicy ass, huh?"* Then he got the attention of a guy beside him, gestured at me and said, *"Tell him, don't I got a big-ol ass?"* Fellahs, at that time I was still shell-shocked about his enormous penis... His 'big-ol' ass never re-entered my mind.

EPISODE 5...

Another day came in prison while on the yard, during extracurricular activity. At this time, hundreds of inmates of all races and cultures walk around and intermingle with one another. All of a sudden, there was a violent fight amongst many inmates, after a few moments the guards contained the violence, ordered all the inmates to line-up across, get butt-naked, ready to spread-'em and cough.

This was embarrassing. I wanted to see all the other inmates, to sorta compare myself, but I didn't want to be seen. By the size of some other guys, I knew they didn't want to be seen either. My penis appeared to be smaller than most of the guys. Of course, I beat out a few of the guys in some races, but not that many. From my experience, I'd say racial penis myths are only around 35% true. Penis comparison could be one of the worst things to happen to an insecure man in regular life. But in prison, revelation of a small penis could humble one of the hardest gang members to lower his voice, slump his shoulders, head and back, and to drop his intimidating walk-about. And at the same time, a more nerdy guy who revealed a bigger than normal penis can be noticed speaking louder, engaging in more activities, and walking-about with a little swagger. Doing hard time was bad enough, but constantly being subjected to strip searches was the worst. From that time on, my penis envy & insecurity really started to fester, and I became angry. **That anger and obsession was fuel and motivation to write about it. And now I hope this can help other men who feel the same way...**

PENIS ENVY...

I almost think it's natural to have...penis envy, that is. And I believe most men with average-to-small size penises have it, or suffer from it. But the men who don't, appear to have more confidence in themselves, live happier lives, and don't get stressed-out as often. It also follows on the flip-side with women; the women with the smallest breasts always seems to be sorta angry, have mood swings, and are often agitated. And though small tits are a huge issue with women, it's not a big issue with men. Many guys could care less.

On the other hand, a small penis could very well be a big issue with women, and a huge issue with men. One reason being; 'this is a Man's world'... and no matter what the penis size be, it'll always be bigger than any big-tit woman could ever be...

Yeah, big tits are nice, but a big dick is King! And everybody knows it. Reason is, a big penis is Power! It always assumes power. And it is often granted power, even if the beholder has no real power.

A large penis is very dangerous! Hard not to believe it be a blessing and a curse... But definitely a weapon of choice. By just the thought of it women swoon with rapturous emotion. They want to see it, they want to touch it, they want to fondle it. And yes, they want to kiss it, suck it, and get fucked by it! The reality of it is, when it comes to women and a big penis, power is implied without prior performance. Its mere presence is compelling to women. It involuntarily forces them in the position they naturally want to be: weakened, humbled, and subjected... If it were up to women, no man with a little penis could ever be a leader in our country, or even rule in second-command. If women knew a little dick was representing, most would probably become unruly and disorderly. At the mere mention of politics, women would be annoyed and could never become interested, even in old age.

When women head down to the poles, they're likely to always vote for or re-elect the official who's tall, cute, has strong handsome features, or has been accused of being a womanizer. The latter, of course, would imply a big penis. You also have those women who walk in the circles of "status attained" men looking to earn a spot, or rather yet, "bump" another girl out of the number-one-spot. This transition of women has labeled the guy as a playboy, or a womanizer. Thing is, these so-called womanized victims know all too well of his ill behavior. But that big dick is more powerful than their disappointment. Therefore, they align themselves with that big dick, but often stick around a little too long and get publicly linked. Still in all, women hate to get played on, but will always love a player! Like I said before, *"a big dick is King"*, and who better to lead a great Country than the King?

Women, liken manly leadership qualities to a sexual connotation. And of course, when they envision this type of man they wish to believe he has a nice aggressive dick that will painfully but pleasurably whip them into submission, so that they may follow without question. And little to no resistance... It is the assumption of sexual prowess with that "whip" known as a big penis that breaks down a woman's resistances. And men know this better than women. But while women tend to view the man as a "whole", men seem to only focus on the penis as being the prize! Whether this mental behavior has merit, or is absurd, is irrelevant. For men, it is this sick preoccupation with the penis that drives behavior. Penis Envy, it is... Nothing but Penis Envy.

As I said before, *a large penis is very dangerous!* It has gotten many men hated, envied and coveted. And it has gotten many men killed, hung and castrated. Penis Envy, it is... Nothing but Penis Envy. It is said: *"The man with the most expensive toys wins the girls"*. (Or, just more like a chance to talk with the girls). But it is known: *"The man with the big penis gets to make love to the girls"*. The playing field is uneven... One man has to work very hard just to get a chance to talk with the girls. The other man is well-endowed and has to learn how to turn down the girls. You see, guys, a woman can sense a man with a big dick like a man can sense rejection from a pretty girl. But it is usually the three *other* attributes that might give her a tale-tale sign of his well endowment; extreme confidence, blatant arrogance, and a bad attitude. Yeah, a bad attitude. In many cases, this guy is a fuckin' jerk! But the girls like it. They can't stop thinking about this type of guy, and they for surely can't stop talking about him.

Confidence in and of itself has always been a sexy turn-on for women. They love it when a man has a strong belief in his ability. Arrogance is just a distant cousin to confidence. It shows experience in "been there, done that", with bragging rights to boot. A slight arrogance is always beneficial around women; it makes them 'shut the fuck up and pay attention!' And last, a bad attitude... Now, does a man with a bad attitude translate to having a big penis? No. But what it does do is put the woman in self-check mode. It makes her feel weak, uneasy, and walk 'on eggshells'. It makes her check her approach, and her choice of words. And it forces her in a subordinate position. All in all, it makes her scared of him... I once heard a woman say, *"In order for me to give a man some pussy, he'd have to scare me a little."*

On another occasion, in a stand-up comedy club, a woman in the first row repeatedly answered her cell phone. This agitated the female comedian. The female comedian stated, *"Who the fuck does he think he is? Keep calling you while I'm doing my routine! Girl, don't he know you at a comedy club? The next time he calls let me answer it!"* She paused a moment, then shouted, *"And He Better Have A Big Ass Dick!"* Needless to say, he did call back; the comedian did answer, and made jokes out of the whole thing. Thing about it is this; the female comedian couldn't stand to see the power that man had over her to repeatedly answer the phone during her entertainment night out. So she internalized the act on herself and concluded, 'there's only one thing that could make me tolerate a man's bullshit, and that is, a Big Dick.'

Penis envy, ma man, penis envy...

Now at the other end of penis envy is nothing to smile about. For the black man it has been nothing but a hidden focus for hate and envy with men of other races. It has begotten them continued discrimination. And it is the root cause of social racism. Men of other races can say what they want. Truth is, most are afraid of the black man for one reason only: perception of a large penis. This physical characteristic of *some* men in one group has managed to influence *most* men in other groups to extreme penis envy, and ultimate penis obsession. This preoccupation with someone else's dick has run amuck in just about every aspect of male and female relations. Job, profession, and corporate industry. Cultural, sexual, and social industry. Other races are accustomed to ownership, being in-charge of large and small groups of men, and being appointed to positions to delegate, officiate, and hire & fire.

Although the need for self preservation and maintaining prominent social status over black men have been great incentives for their continued rule, it however, pales in comparison with the sheer driving force of an obsessed mental preoccupation they hoard for black men, his physique, his elite physical ability, and his profound penis. The latter of which has the power to negatively influence the most powerful of men, and quail the snobbery of the most prestigious woman.

In the past, a small group of white men known as the KKK has allowed the size of a black man's penis to mentally derange them to the point of committing frequent acts of castration and mutilation on black men, hanging them by their penis, or random senseless murder on black men and boys.

Although today's hate and fear of black men is less obvious and violent, many social ramifications are still ardently practiced; from just getting a regular job to getting admittance to a preferred school. From joining an elite club, to fraternizing with a select group. And the handed down practice of white flight. It is all too apparent that white people (Asians included) will do whatever it takes (even to financial hardship) to keep from living in or close to the area of black people. From the continued practice of the parents financing their kids education, and allowing them to live at home at no expense. To a huge jump-start by handing down the house to their kids in an already white neighborhood, while they retire to a nicer area. Or, more whites independently taking second jobs as their motivation. They just do whatever they need to do in "order" to keep their little daughter as far away from the black man as possible. And they do treat it as an "order!".

Many white people would much rather struggle with two jobs to pay ridiculous high rent or mortgage in an expensive area, than to live merely "affordable" in a community with 10% or more blacks. The latter of which would be like, *rolling the dice...* 'Six' & 'Ace' – save the bar, nobody wins... or worse, craps – 'Snake Eyes', that is... either the white people just straight out lose, or their daughter gets to see his *snake*... And if this is allowed whether physical or just visual, a curious interest in black men could develop – with a lack of interest in white men to follow... Either way, stills their motivation out of those neighborhoods. But white flight could also be due to the lower property values and their slower rate of increase, inferior school programs and education, higher neighborhood crime rate and an overall intimidation and safety concern lurking around the neighborhood. How could you blame them? I wouldn't want to live there either...

Somebody better start *Black Flight*!

PART I:
SMALL PENIS 101

1. Accept The Fact That You Have A Small Penis.

My first suggestion is definitely one of the most difficult to take heed of. It's just too personal with us. Impossible to just sit back and accept it without a fight. Anyhow, in order to move forward and start accepting yourself, you must first knock off every standard that society (especially women) dictate you must measure up to, physically and sexually. This is because our self-acceptance and mental and physical well-being have so much to do with our relations with other people, and our perception of societal views.

Remember, even though we humans have freedom of choice, we weren't granted the freedom to choose what we look like. And most people don't like the looks they were born with. Ask anyone. They'll tell you many things they'd love to change about themselves.

But the important thing is most people eventually accept themselves for who they are. Basically because they've acknowledged they have absolutely no say-so and no control in the matter. So control what you can, and forget about what you can't. Live to live by this cardinal rule: focus your energies on improving what you can about yourself, realistically. That is, all things within reason. Stop wasting vast amounts of your creative and positive energy worrying about the rest. Give yourself the best gift you can: self-love. Because self-healing requires self-love. And the most subtle but effective level of self-love is when you can use it to combat society's dictates and perceptions.

So cancel that mental trip and start living a healthy sex life. Remember, you love pussy just as much as the next man. And you don't see him trippin' ...little dick or not.

2. *Know What* Not *To Do During Sex.*

Believe it or not, knowing your sexual *'don'ts'* is even more to your advantage than knowing your sexual *'dos'*. Most women will agree that a man who pushes all the right buttons is a great thing. And probably all would also agree that a man who pushes just a few of the wrong buttons can turn a great thing into a not-so-great-thing – even a sexual disaster!

Sexual experiences are akin to daily life experiences: we all remember the good times... but we can never forget the bad times. And those bad times, even though sometimes few and far between, are experiences that tend to stick out, outweigh and override the good experiences. And during intimacy and sex, this is one time when 'one bad apple can spoil the whole barrel'.

Memories of major sexual *'don'ts'* can influence a woman's mind and emotions to the degree that anything resembling or associated with the bad act is immediately rejected. And because some of these *'don'ts'* are experienced during sex exclusively, it can turn off a woman's desire for the entire sex act. Completely!

For the man with the small-penis complex who is trying to make a good impression, this is valuable information, and may be exactly what the sex doctor ordered. It should be kept in mind that different actions turn off different women, and to different degrees. And that even some so-called *'bad acts'* can be right on time, or even turn-ons for other women.

However, my intention is to be more general and express some of the common complaints women have against men during sex; things which women are reluctant to address, and usually (for fear of hurting the man's feelings), would never speak out against directly:

1. *Don't be a rough Nipple-Pincher & -Puller.*

Men are very visual creatures! And to see a woman's breasts naked, or even scantily-clad, can be most potent in triggering sexual arousal and erotic charge. The sight and feel of a woman's breast stimulates a man so much, he sometimes gets too rough – hard stroking on her nipples, harder sucking, even biting! Problem is, for many women (even around half of all women) this rough behavior hurts and is often very painful. Reason being, the breast, nipple and areola (the darker ring that encircles the nipple) are all richly endowed with nerve endings, causing them to be very sensitive to the touch, even tender! So be very gentle. 'Cause what you think is passion play could be annoying as hell, and turn enjoyment into instant discomfort.

2. _Don't pull on her hair to yank her head back._

For some prehistoric or animalistic reason, when some men enter their mate from the rear, they tend to get the urge to grab the top of her hair, pulling and yanking her head back; (This is the greatest! I'm with ya on this guys! But it could pose a problem...) This behavior doesn't necessarily hurt, but to some women it's a mental degrader... They don't want to be treated like an animal, so they say...

Women don't really mind being dominated and controlled during sex, but they also don't necessarily like when he plays cowboy tryin' to break a wild mustang!

3. _Don't be a stuffer._

This means trying to stuff a limp penis into a vagina. Men usually try this method in attempt to gain a quicker erection shortly after they've become limp from ejaculation. Although the intention is honorable, these seemingly endless efforts very seldom work. It's not the thirty minute to an hour it takes to get an erection that annoys women, but the fact that this method is a constant stop-and-go because the penis keeps falling out. Not to mention the valuable wasted time that could've been spent on intimate foreplay!

4. _Don't be a pelvic pounder._

First of all, you're not the king of _'Bang-Her Hill'_! Second of all, all this banging and pounding could soon start to hurt, which will definitely detract from her pleasure from your penis, making her pull back with every anticipation of your pelvic thrusts. But perhaps the best reason for not banging so hard is, you don't want her to think you are trying to overcompensate for having a little penis, do you?

5. _Women don't like this 'head shoving' shit!_ Don't keep forcing her head down gesturing her to perform oral sex. Men usually do this to women who won't perform fellatio, are reluctant to do it or won't voluntarily do it on their own. And gesturing her to do something she doesn't want to will turn her off from you all the way! She may have her own insecurities or hesitations about performing for you. Give her a chance to surprise you when she feels comfortable, or if she really is avoiding it, bring it up for discussion at a more neutral time.

6. _Don't keep asking a woman throughout the sex act, "Do you feel it?"_

This is a question often repeated by a man with a small-penis complex. If you keep asking, she'll know you're insecure about your penis size. How 'bout you ask yourself, _'can you feel it?'_ And if your answer is _'not really'_, then guess what Einstein, she can't either...

7. And probably the worst thing you could do is ask her: _"Did you have an orgasm?"_

Wow, dude! Another bonehead outta turn question. Any questions you have for her like that should only be asked _after_ you've asked _yourself_ a couple manhood challenging questions, like; _'Can my ego handle a negative answer?'_ Or, _'Am I so confident I gave a stellar performance to the point I don't give a damn whether she got hers or not?'_ But, what if you like the girl... can you really handle some ill-truth? Let me tell ya, women don't like lying, but often will to spare a man's ego. Just don't make her mad! 'Cause that same question will be held against you, later on...

These last two _'don'ts'_ (#6 & 7) reveal sexual immaturity and emotional instability. You'd be wise to avoid them.

3. Become Less Sexually Inhibited.

As long as it doesn't conflict with your religious and/or personal morals, one needs to practice not holding back during sexual intercourse. Don't keep forbidding your body from experiencing sexual actions longed for. Deprive not the body/brain system of feeling erotic physical pleasures, nor sensual mental stimulation. Termination of any inkling of mental inhibition must be strictly enforced in order to free the mind and allow the brain to transmit intimate nerve signals into physical sensations.

4. Massage Your Genitalia With Body Oils.

One of the problems many men with small penises share is that they also don't very much like their penises. Therefore, other than urinating and occasional sex, they rarely show their penis any special attention. No touching, no massaging, and no pampering. They'd just as soon not even look at it, unless examining for a genital infection. This great dislike for one's penis could lead to something worse, like self-hate. One way of helping the problem is to face it head on (no pun intended). Although a penis may appear small, it never falls short of providing its owner with maxim pleasure in the sensitive area.

So, for all he does for you, show your appreciation by rewarding him with some quality time. You know, do the male bonding thing... and I'm not necessarily talking about masturbating to ejaculation, but more or less developing a physical relationship with your penis.

Fact of the matter is, you guys are more than just a mere part of each other; you share a most unique bond, by medium of blissful feelings that enrapture the mind and body – a physical state unequalled in human perception. So, neglect him not.

Cultivate that bond. Stimulate that bond by touching and gently rubbing and slowly stroking your penis. Massage lotions and body oils on your penis. It will thank you by first totally relaxing within itself, looking longer and appearing fuller – more pleasing to the beholder. Stroking and massaging the penis with body oils will also relax the mind and body of its owner, all the while delivering light pleasures and sensations.

By often engaging in this activity one will develop a more favorable relation between his penis and himself. Thereby enjoying his penis and becoming less preoccupied about the size of it.

5. Enter Sex With The Intention To Please One Another. Many Times, Your Goal Dictates Your Performance.

The mind is an incredible gift. And it has the potential and ability to influence and manipulate its owner into just about any mind-set. Desiring a great sex performance is no exception.

Even though sex seems mostly physical, it's actually more mental. For many men who feel they have a small penis, anticipation of a sexual encounter with a woman can be very fretful and worrisome – largely because he mostly defines his manhood by the size of his penis.

Even though, for the most part, a woman will never show concern about his size, he sincerely believes the woman finds his small penis as something to quietly ridicule. And this kind of low sexual esteem and uncertain feelings about her can dramatically hinder a man's sexual response and sexual performance.

That is why men who feel bad in any way about their penis being too small should practice methods to bring about a change in the perception of their own sexuality. The objective is to approach sex with the intention of just trying to please one another and enjoy one another. Because many times, it's your goal that dictates your performance.

But fortunately for less well-endowed men, women, for the most part, don't see a man as just a penis, unlike a lot of men who see a woman as a pair of breasts and a vagina. And don't forget, when a woman enters a sex act with a man, her intentions are probably more so to please him than they are to please herself. This is just keeping in line with a woman's basic nature: to give of herself to satisfy and please her man, while feeling more love for him and gaining more attachment to him in the process.

So take comfort in these facts about women, and ease yourself of the emotional stress of having a small penis. Spare your mind the mental anguish of anticipating a poor sexual performance. Enter the realm of intercourse with a new level of intimacy. One that creates close bonds and encourages affection - but doesn't emphasize insecurities.

Redundant questions like *"Can you feel it?"* overemphasize a man's insecurities and begins a woman's curiosity; does he have such insecurities? The last thing you want to do during sexual intercourse is derail a woman's pleasure by questioning your own performance – even if your desire is to please her. A woman instinctively knows that she cannot be effective in pleasing her man if the man has physical and emotional hang-ups that involve her, and are even more so stimulated by her. This is one sure way to diminish a woman's sense of security and well-being in the relationship, and could be the primary cause of sudden break-up, separation, divorce, or at the least the beginning of a self-inflicted rocky relationship.

Even though generally it doesn't take much to get a man aroused (especially on first erection) falling victim to performance anxiety could turn ordinary attempts at erection into a mentally and physically laborious job. So at least try to clear yourself of the mental aspect, because it is the mental dysfunction that turns getting an erection into a chore that must be accomplished quickly and with little effort to carry out the mission, conquer the woman emotionally and fulfill her sexual desire.

Any time it's too much a struggle, try concentrating on the gentle and subtle joys of foreplay and intimacy. This will help you both relax and allow your lovemaking to unfold more naturally.

So just enter the sex encounter with strong intentions to please her and have fun doing it. You could bet her intentions will be the same. Having this attitude is much safer and less stressful, because when you get rid of the performance anxiety, you automatically reduce the pressure significantly, which in turn affords you (at least) a better chance at a satisfactory performance. Then, if you still fail at your performance, count your lucky stars you're not all bummed out – because you didn't take it that seriously in the first place.

6. Don't Let Premature Ejaculation Be Another Reason To Run Her Off.

Let's face it, ask just about any woman how she'd feel about having sexual relations with a man with a little penis and almost always you'll get a negative response.

But if you turn around and asked the same women, "What if you didn't have a choice in the matter, then how would you feel?" And more often than not, you will get an answer similar to, "Well, as long as he could maintain an erection for a good while, I could deal with it." Listen up fellahs, the women say they "could" deal with it! And when women say they could deal with a man's small penis, they are in essence saying: "This is not my preference, but I could get content." So, now, we men must seek practical methods to combat this sudden ejection of semen happening too early before the desired time, called premature ejaculation. It is a detested annoyance that physically afflicts and emotionally troubles millions of men globally.

One thing most of these men who suffer from premature ejaculation have in common is that they all want so desperately to be able to satisfy a woman! Even if it means not being satisfied himself with his own orgasm. In all actuality, as long as he can bring the woman to climax once, or better yet, twice during the sexual encounter, that man will be very satisfied and pleased with his performance. And the woman will feel gratified and want to give of herself to him again.

7. Use Safe Numbing Creams Or Sprays Before Intercourse.

As if the mentally devastating effects of being aware that women don't want a man with a small penis wasn't enough, another major problem seems to plague us all the more: premature ejaculation. We just get off too quick. And with some of us, we cum just within a few strokes!

This is an ongoing problem that seems to happen with every sexual encounter without fail. Our premature ejaculation is such a sure-fire thing, we'd bet our life on it. One comforting thing to remember: millions of men throughout the world suffer from premature ejaculation. And this condition is not limited to any particular life style, race, culture, or penis size.

One common solution to this problem is to de-sensitize the head of the penis a little (or a lot) so sexual intercourse won't feel as good. This could be accomplished by the practical method of desensitizing the head of the penis by the use of a numbing cream or spray. One popular spray is called 'Stay Hard'. These products are applied directly to the head of the penis. And within minutes, they weaken or deprive the penis head of the intense feeling for a short while, (depending on the strength of the product and the amount applied). But this 'short while' could be all the time needed for her to reach a climax and for some of his self-esteem to be restored. (Note: the use of numbing products is usually done without the woman's prior knowledge, in an attempt for the man to protect his self-esteem and/or sense of masculinity.) These products and others similar to it can be purchased from a doctor (urologist), and over the counter. They are also available in stores that cater to sexual needs.

8. Don't Develop Performance Anxiety Because Of It.

In so many cases, men with small penises allow what they feel is a purely physical problem to develop into a full-blown psychological problem: performance anxiety. For an otherwise physically able and sexually capable man, out of all the things that can go wrong before and during sex, one of the worst is performance anxiety.

Performance anxiety is probably the most common cause of poor sexual performance and sexual dysfunction in men who have small-penis complexes. Continuous and uncontrolled performance anxiety is a very serious problem and should never be taken lightly. And the fact that it's mostly mental makes it very effective at dealing a deathblow to sexual satisfaction. Performance anxiety usually shows itself just before sex, by way of the man not being able to obtain an erection. And if he doesn't get an erection almost immediately or at least within fifteen minutes of when he thinks she's ready for penetration, he quickly remembers failed past experiences when he couldn't get an erection. And his mind begins to worry that he won't be able to get an erection no matter what he does, nor how great the desire.

All too often, and once again, sexual satisfaction is delayed – physically for her, and mentally for him. Men who suffer from small-penis complex often obsess over the idea of pleasing the woman. This, in its own right, is a good thing; but couple in the factor with performance anxiety and you get a sexual nightmare – a formula for overwhelming mental and emotional devastation. A mental state that persists, and is extremely difficult to get rid of, even through logic and reasoning. It can even develop into an extreme case - to where whenever confronted with the possibility of sex he simply can't and won't get an erection. This is mainly because all his fears and anxieties from failed past performances continue to plague and haunt his mind, diminishing the sexual libido, and causing exaggerated self-doubt, lack of confidence and self-induced mental abuse. These demons work together to negatively but powerfully overwhelm sexual desire and the body's natural impulses for sex.

Instead of viewing sex as a man and a woman coming together most privately to make love and share with each other their inmost intimate physical beings, men who suffer greatly from performance anxiety tend to see sex as a do-or-die situation in which his penis could get whacked off if he doesn't obtain an erection within 10 minutes.

Or he views sex as a pressured performance, as if he was batter-up in the bottom of the ninth in the World Series, with bases loaded! Wow! C'mon man... what ordinary man is expected to produce a miracle erection under that kind of pressure? None in my time, I hope.

In order to have an erection and continue on to sexual satisfaction, the man must first try to rid himself of past memories of failed attempts and rotten performances; and he must rid his body and mind of undue tensions and sexual inhibitions, in order that he might relax. But total relaxation shouldn't be the goal, remember, a rigid erection is the objective. Therefore a few passion butterflies in the stomach are always helpful to get things started.

An important thing to remember is that sex should be something that men enjoy. After all, sex is a huge and frequent part of their lives; therefore, men mustn't allow their minds to be filled with worries about their erection and giving a stellar performance in bed. It's not that serious – to women either.

Even though, generally it doesn't take a man much to get aroused (especially on first erection), falling victim to performance anxiety could turn ordinary attempts at erection into a mentally and physically laborious job! The fact is, if you have trouble maintaining an erection, or worse still, take too long (20 min. or longer) regaining an erection, and this type of behavior happens to be a woman's first impression, or tends to occur frequently, it could ruin a prospective relationship.

So at least try to clear yourself of the mental aspect. Because it is the mental dysfunction that turns an erection into something we must perform; something that is ordered, and we must execute and complete; something that we must accomplish with little effort in order to carry out the mission; and something that we men must quickly achieve in order to conquer the woman emotionally and fulfill her every sexual desire. If all this fails or is too much of a struggle, then I suggest you communicate to your mate to be very patient with you during sex with no pressure for immediate erection. And just concentrate on gentle and subtle joys of intimacy and foreplay.

9. Learn How To Massage A Woman.

So what, your sex performances aren't all that great. And some of your best ones you swore by – she didn't even acknowledge! Most likely, you blamed it on having a little penis. And if she didn't climax, chances are, she did too. We men with less length and girth on our penis want nothing more in the world than for a woman to be satisfied with our performance. We so much want woman to need us sexually. Need us to touch them intimately. And need us to caress them sensually. But most of all we desire them to scream, *"Encore!"* after sex.

Well, don't despair, 'cause with a little patience and training on how to massage a woman you could earn some of your desire – at least, she'll welcome another chance after a poor first performance.

Let's face it, everyone loves a good massage. And afterwards, we always feel grateful, and totally indebted to the giver. We all have a basic know-how on rubbing other's bodies to make them feel more relaxed. But when tending a woman's fragile body, some special attention needs to be given that only proper training could provide.

You'll become invaluable to her by being able to totally relax her into a state of serenity by using your hands to stimulate full circulation in neglected areas. Using your knuckles, palms and finger tips to press and penetrate deep into skin-folds. Delicately, but effectively squeezing and pinching muscles, loosening joints, helping her body to feel supple. Enabling her to relieve tension and pent-up frustration. Believe me, after that performance she'll feel indebted to you for life! And in her mind you can't be replaced by nothing and no one. Then, take a look at her face... The demand for *"Encore!"* will be written all over it!

10. Double Your Normal Foreplay Time.

Nothing stimulates a woman's emotional sex desire like foreplay! Nothing prompts and primes her sexually submissive gestures like foreplay! And nothing excites her raging sex driven hormones quite like foreplay! What exactly is foreplay? Heh-heh...

Who's to say? Simple but vague definition: Those various acts of mutual sexual stimulation that go before sexual intercourse. Foreplay is a quality process that women have always wanted, and crave dearly – even without intercourse. They like it visual, physical, emotional, and they love it to be mental. They love it to be mental because women love to be seduced. And they know if done properly, foreplay yields the ultimate seduction of the mind! And although women will never tell you, they love nothing more than a man who successfully challenges her emotional mentality into sexually stimulating thoughts. These stimulating thoughts are crucial to a woman's sexual satisfaction. For women, mental foreplay is somewhat like a game, in which her sole objective is emotional surrender. She tries to win, and very well could win, yet doesn't want to win. Reason being, she so wants to reward him for his efforts, yet also needs her lover to understand that making love is as much a mental endeavor as it is a physical performance.

If he internalizes this method she will allow herself to be turned on and overtaken by his actions. In turn, he will realize that the surest way to give his woman sexual pleasure and emotional fulfillment is to first seduce her mind rather than speed-race to her body. Men must keep in mind that a woman's biological make-up is different than theirs. Consequently, her mental perceptions differ also.

His greatest aphrodisiac is through his sense of vision: ogling the female body. Her greatest aphrodisiac is through her sense of hearing; feeling his masculine words penetrates her emotions. Therefore, she won't have it any other way! To gain total satisfaction, she needs a little something more... She must have mental foreplay before giving him physical body play. With women, sex starts with the mind, and her mood – though it's sometimes peculiar and not easily detected.

This strange and challenging characteristic also works to her advantage; for he spends more quality time fondling her body, all the while coaxing and cajoling her in a low seductive voice. All this is nothing but extended foreplay, but women are very turned on by it! It really turns her on to see a man so patient and considerate; one who acknowledges her slow starts, and places her feelings before his own. And a man who takes his time to stimulate her emotionally as well as sexually. She gets all this pleasure and gratification simply from his soothing and caressing touch, his inviting gestures and his emotionally sensitive words. And NONE of which have anything to do with a penis or the size of it, because making love involves much more than one's mechanical abilities. So, if you have a little penis and don't think you're all that great in bed, then improve your overall lovability quotient, simply by doubling your normal foreplay time. Because memorable sex is what women always come back to…and it begins with foreplay.

11. Make Love Like A Lesbian.

This one you really have to get into to feel what I'm talking about. Because it requires a lot of time, a lot of patience and a lot of giving. And because most men have very little to no experience at it, they find it difficult to accept the delay of self-gratification through penetration.

At first, making love like a lesbian could become very frustrating for men and even lead to no interest in sex this way... mainly because it reduces the role of male aggression and dims the spotlight of his greatest sexual achievement – the Erection! However, this could do wonders for the man who's penis-insecure.

Men generally think that if they're not serving her the *'hot-rod'*, what could possibly be more pleasing or satisfaction-giving...? Well, how about an act of intimacy – with one who knows a woman's body and is well-acquainted with a woman's feelings. Hard as it is to admit to, women know us better than we know ourselves. And they most certainly know women better than we do. So why not take lessons form the expert: another woman?

You ever see two lesbians goin' at it? Or better yet, ever tried to pull one woman away from her lesbian lover and found nothing but resistance or a cold verbal let-down? You might have slightly better odds at snatching away a raw steak from a hungry lion because these girls ain't havin' it! And if you ain't never had a sharp taste of a woman bringing the bitch out in her, then brace yourself, 'cause you finna experience it firsthand. And it's not necessarily your fault you just haven't been brought up to speed. And at this point, I don't believe either one of them is up for giving you a crash course. So until then, just pop in another video of DEBBIE DOES DONNA and take notes. When a woman shuns you for another woman it's probably because she felt there was nothing you could do for her. Or more to the point, she feels that you do not know how to go about addressing her emotional feelings and feminine needs. And as you know, everything is about *feelings* to a woman. They are governed by emotion. And when it comes to intimacy and sex, feelings are running high. That is when a woman is most vulnerable.

In these times of intimacy between two women, each instinctively competes with the other in paying particular attention to the innermost feelings they share. They do this not only by being very familiar with each other's character and body, but just as important, they gladly and willingly spend as much time pleasing the other and trying to bring her to satisfaction.

With men, it's not so much the lack of knowledge of the woman, but more so the lack of understanding that a woman's pleasure and ultimate satisfaction is wrapped-up in *time*. And this *time* usually translates into much more than the guy is used to. So the man (before he cums on himself) responds by slipping her the penis – a sure way to his satisfaction, assuming hers too.

Problem is, his hurried response could be a big mistake where she's concerned. Once again, she's deprived of her time. She feels cheated of the closeness and gratification she gets when a man is in to her... IN TO HER. She wants to feel, *'He is in to me'*... Sadly, it goes without saying; she's cheated again of intimacy. Her intimate satisfaction requires the feelings she experiences when your warm skin is against hers, and not just grabbing for her hot spots. Her entire body requires more exploration through touch. Her ears require all the sexual *oohs* and *ahhs* and compliments you should give throughout foreplay, the sex act, and pillow-talk afterwards. And her mind desires your empathy for her vulnerability during these heightened emotions.

So gentleman, do yourself a huge favor and take your attention (where you think her attention is) – off your penis! And put it where it should be... on her... Just how lesbians do it…

12. Make Love To A Woman's Erogenous Zones.

Even if you do have a little penis, one sure-fire way to compensate for your size is to *make love to a woman's erogenous zones*! I guarantee you, play around these sensuous areas and your sexual performance will be without fail! The after effects of this experience will leave your woman in total relaxation, total satisfaction, and pleasant anticipation – yearning for more each and *every* time you make love. If you're consistent enough in giving her this highly sensitive treatment (maybe even as little as once a week), your little penis size won't ever be an issue of concern. Instead, she will view your sexuality as a whole and think of it as exquisite and of the highest quality.

Just what are erogenous zones? Those specific areas of the body that are erotically stimulated through sensuous contact. Areas like the clitoris, the nipples, the ear lobes, the outer surface of the anus, the inner and outer lips of the vagina, the lips and tongue, the nape of neck, the inner thighs, and of course the entrance of the vagina – all of which are highly sensitive and can arouse erotically when touched, kissed, licked or fondled. Make love to these erogenous zones and her heart and emotions will rate you a cut above. She will reminisce lovingly of your technique on carefully and elaborately exploring her body. And she will think of your performance as sharply intense, yet beautiful, delicate and highly refined!

Just to note, a woman could have an erogenous zone anywhere… and it's not necessarily limited to those listed here. Her erogenous zones can even vary with mood change. And their individual sensitivity can also vary – even as often as day to day. So you see, it's gonna take some attentive and observing effort on your part to discern her moods, responses, behavior and her sexuality.

Most women hold a silent complaint against men for not being more aware and sensitive to their erogenous zones. In most cases she will hold her complaint as just that: silent. This is because a woman will go the extra mile, and then some, in order to protect her man's fragile ego. But only for so long... Because if a woman is used to becoming aroused by being stimulated in a certain way (whether it was from you or someone else before you), and that stimulation is neglected (knowingly or unknowingly), the woman can develop pent-up frustration. Her attitude will eventually manifest itself physically. She might pull back her body in a rejecting manner during sex or intimate foreplay every time you initiate some stimulation that's not her desire. Or her attitude can manifest itself verbally through indirect statements of concern just before sex; sarcastic words and remarks during sex and during pillow-talk shortly after sex, or worse, no verbal response at all after sex during pillow-talk hour.

Women enjoy having a man who is patient in giving complete and thorough pleasure to a woman's body. And not so quick to pleasure his own self by thrusting his penis into her vagina. It makes her feel beautiful and wanted when a man takes his time with her body and is creative in trying new ways to thrill her. It makes her feel especially feminine, irresistible, and utterly desirable when her man constantly, and unprovokingly licks and kisses her body over and over again, from the bottom of her feet to the soft moist inner thighs up to the thin skin around her neck – while placing extra emphasis on her prime erogenous zones.

Men who have good intentions by trying to be creative should keep this in mind: be careful of spending too much time trying to create a brand new erogenous zone on your woman's body... just because that spot worked on another woman doesn't mean it'll work on her. If she doesn't verbally express sexual *oohs* and *ahhs* or sensual sighs within the first 30 seconds then it's not a hot spot! Quickly move on to the next area of choice. Because if you stay there too long, or persist in doing it in just about every sexual encounter with her, she'll start to think you've been using this technique on another woman and now are trying it on her. This could spark immediate jealousy and anger, because she will swear your mind is on the other woman and the intimacy you both share is not exclusively hers. If by chance this does enter her mind (and it will) it could ruin sexual excitement for her – or at least put a damper on it – and on your relations with her.

Just remember... the clitoris is an unmistakable erogenous zone for most women. Both the head and shaft of the clitoris are richly endowed with nerve endings, and therefore highly sensitive to touch. The inner lips of the vagina are richly supplied with nerve endings also. And don't forget about the highly sensitive entrance of the vagina just above and outside the vaginal opening, as well as the first couple of inches.

And try your luck at finding the "G" spot. Apply pressure on the roof of her vagina a few inches beyond the opening... If she responds like never before – great! If she looks at you like you're crazy, ABANDON MISSION!!

13. During Sex, Close Her Legs And You Will Feel More Friction.

Although there are a lot of men in the world with small penises, many are quite good in bed - at least their women think so. And because after sex, their women almost always appear totally satisfied, these men don't feel insecure about their sexual abilities. Some of these men even have a small-penis complex, but they don't suffer from it!

Instead of having a big penis, they try and make up for it in other areas that the woman desires, like being fun in bed, flipping and twisting her in different mounting positions, and keeping staying power throughout the entire erotic act. But in spite of all these accomplishments, and in spite of the fact that she appears totally satisfied, the man with the small penis still tends to feel quite incomplete...

By not having as much bone mass and flesh that increase length and girth naturally possessed by men well-endowed, he sometimes feels deprived of that special frictional touch – that unique fleshy resistance between erogenous surfaces during pelvic thrusts. And if the man has ever experienced this pleasurable friction before, he will always long for it, stopping at nothing to regain that feeling, even if it means leaving his current woman to find it.

But if the man is in love with his lady, doesn't plan on leaving her, yet still craves more sexual friction, I strongly suggest this: during sexual intercourse, close her legs and you will feel more friction and total closure of pussy around your penis. It really works! And it's quite fun! Kinda erotic, too.

There could be many ways to perform this. I will attempt to explain two:

Step One: lay her flat on her back with her heels kicked straight in the air, touching each other.

Step two. Now that you have succeeded in getting her to recline in the horizontal fashion, you immediately… Well, I'm confident you can figure out the rest. This position can be pretty inviting because it feels good and you're in control. You could hold her legs tightly together, open them at will, or get creative and twist them closed. Either way, you derive maximum friction.

Another practical position is to lay her flat on her stomach with her arms stretched forward and feet together. Her arms are stretched forward so when you mount her from the rear you can lie on top of her while lovingly holding her hands. This will give her added emotional intimacy. Of course, there are other positions for even more stimulating methods, but I do believe they require a few more *inches*. So don't get too carried away, just stick to these for now.

But I guarantee you, if you want an easy sensible way to feel more friction from penis-vagina bumping and grinding, then close her legs. You will no doubt experience the sensational feeling of your penis resistively penetrating her wet warm fleshy, pussy-folds of skin. She'll feel it too! – and be excited by your sense of initiative and creativity in bed.

PART II:

LIVING WITH A SMALL PENIS

14. Stop Worrying About It!

The first thing you need to know is that worrying about it isn't good for anything, especially your mental state. Worrying about it could bring on much unwanted stress that will, without a doubt, hinder your ability to deal and/or cope with yourself in life's daily activities. Worrying about it contributes a great deal to our feeling that something most essential to our being is incomplete; therefore we feel inadequate, less sexy and unwanted. And the hair thinning process could result from undue worrying about it, not to mention unexpected gray hairs.

15. Always Remember: It's Usually Not As Bad As We Think.

As the saying goes, *"The grass is always greener on the other side."*

Why do we believe the grass is always greener on the other side? Is it just sheer human nature to desire what you don't yourself possess? Is it that intriguing optimistic curiosity that ever-plagues us all? Or is it just pure old-fashioned brainwashing that implies, *"You're not good enough until you get what the other guys got"*-?

If we seriously contemplate our situation and ourselves – it's probably the latter. This just goes to show that it's not as bad as we usually think. This holds true for some men with small penises; they have a serious little-dick complex. These particular men swear the world would be a totally better place for them, if only they had a bigger dick! They feel they are the only one among their peers who's suffering. And no one hears or understands their pain. These men blame virtually everything in their lives – personal mishaps, social ills, all past negative sexual experiences, and all their present sexual hang-ups on having a little penis. This may sound a bit far-fetched for some, of course, but for others, it's very true.

And this is not hard to understand, especially if we look at the behavioral effects of more prominent problems our society faces, such as obsession with the female breasts, hair loss, and the never-ending battle with weight and obesity. Check out today's female… preoccupied with her breast size. If they aren't 36C or bigger, she's emotionally uncomfortable and physically dissatisfied. She places all of her worth in her breast size – her social worth, her economic worth, and her sex appeal. She'll even risk permanent deforming results by going under the knife in an attempt to feel better about herself and the hope of a wicked society looking more favorably at her. And this is a generally healthy woman – there's nothing wrong with her or her breast size.

Look at the affects of hair loss on men… to say nothing of hair loss for women, which is on the rise. Could you imagine the mental and emotional turmoil she'd go through knowing she's losing her hair - the major symbol of her feminine beauty?

And how could male-patterned baldness affect a man's behavior and self-worth? Well, he swears up and down he didn't get that job promotion because of his hair loss, and who'd want a balding man representing their company anyway, right? He thinks a woman would never approach him at a party because the first thing she sees is that big bald spot on the back of his head. And he doesn't feel comfortable wearing a baseball cap because soon as he takes it off, people will think he was just trying to cover that receding hairline.

Look at the billion dollars a year spent on hair transplants, toupees, and other related technologies. But why? Male patterned baldness is not a disease. And they're usually not that bald… and some women actually prefer bald men!

And what about all the emotionally ill overweight and obese people suffering on a daily basis? They are forced to live in a society where "thin" always seems to be "in" and are discriminated against in just about every arena society has to offer. When you're overweight, employers refuse to hire you, and the opposite sex barely looks at you, except with ridicule. Even when overweight people just shop for groceries, others often look at them with scorn and disgrace. And to make matters worse, the billions of dollars spent each year on weight-loss programs don't even work. And the ones that do work are so dangerous they tend to have one major side-effect: a possible death sentence!

And you think you got problems just because your penis size is smaller than average? It's not that bad. These people blame absolutely everything on being overweight, and with a lot more cause than you do.

16. Don't Spend TOO Much Time Alone.

One pattern of behavior commonly seen in men who feel self-conscious about their small penis size, is spending too much time alone.

Of these men, some are natural loners while others are not. But both volunteer to take themselves to seclusion. While both types may be seeking solace and comfort, they end up spending excessive time stressing about their condition and wallowing in self- pity.

Great it would be if this personal time alone were spent on building and reinforcing the positive attributes of oneself. But, on the contrary, this particular time often turns to 'down time' where negativity sets in and a self-invalidating process begins.

Sometimes the worst thing one can do for an emotional or physical problem is to dwell on it, the end of which is only depression. One good solution to this problem is to become more family oriented - be it biological or social family. Gravitate toward people who are doing good work and those who seek new adventures. Get out and mingle with people who are go-getters, positive thinkers, and doers. Being around positive people will do wonders to uplift your spirit.

Always remember: *never unplug completely from your social contacts, because excessive dwelling on the self is bound to take over*. While self-care is essential, excessive worry about the self is destructive. Instead, place your energies into developing a creative talent or project that takes your mind off your personal concerns. It will make you feel more present, more accomplished and better about yourself. You can also attend educational or social conferences or take part in community events.

The change of atmosphere and conduct will do you good.

17. Start Loving Yourself More.

Men who suffer from insecurities about their penis size almost always develop a sort of hate for themselves. This feeling of self-disdain is usually one of the first effects of a small-penis complex. Virtually guaranteed to follow is an inferiority complex. Psychologically, this is a neurotic condition resulting from various feelings of inferiority, derived from real or imagined physical, social or sexual inadequacy.

Men suffering from this condition could find it most difficult to *"love themselves more"*. But it must be done. The first step is to rid your mind of the thoughts and feelings attached to an ideal penis size, or the so-called "standard" in society's eye for a man's makeup.

Love yourself... and know that you have a Divine purpose here.

Love yourself... accentuate the greater qualities that people love about you.

Love yourself... give yourself credit for your worth and value.

Love yourself... treat yourself to quality things in life.

Love yourself... keep yourself well groomed and manicured. When you look better you feel better about yourself.

Love yourself... and most of all realize that you are "uniquely different", there is only one of you in all of time; your ways are unique, with your own gifts; you can't be replaced by anything or anyone.

18. *If You Stress About It, Find Someone To Confide In.*

It is often found that men with small penises also stress over sexual insecurities. These insecurities vary in nature. Not only about penis size but also about emotions and activity that occur during the sex act. All of which can appear difficult to understand, much less control, and sometimes leave the man feeling at a loss.

Because the issue is sex and his ability to perform in bed, men internalize these negative feelings weakening themselves, and viewing their manhood in question, often finding no supportive or compensative answers. To combat these feelings of inadequacy, men usually do little or nothing about it – just sulk in it.

One effective alternative to inner withdrawal is turning to someone to talk to, or someone close to confide in. Although not widely publicized or recognized among men, there is much power and emotional self-healing to be found simply by supportive discussion and active listening.

The first step is to choose the person you wish to confide in very carefully and with the utmost discrimination. Look within family and your circle of friends for candidates with whom you get along. Depending on your mental and emotional state, finding someone you trust and are comfortable with can be a difficult and drawn-out task. Luckily, with most people, there is someone in your life who thinks he or she knows you well and can help determine what's best for you. Eliminate those friends who tend to give you the blues. Whether you choose a man or woman is solely up to you, but be sure you trust their discretion and that you sincerely believe he or she can help you improve your situation by listening to you.

This person should be someone who likes and loves you for who you are, one who has proven over time that they accept you with all your flaws, both physical and emotional. The type of person that always sticks by you, and won't give up on you, even when you give up on yourself – that's who you want to go to! Because men with such emotional insecurities need a 'go-to guy.' One of understanding, who will allow the insecure to vent. Without a person of comfort, self- dissatisfaction, self-torture and self-hate will only continue to build, and possibly create a serious mental disorder.

So go to them. But instead of chit-chatting the usual or gossiping about things not in your heart, change the focus. Let them know you want to talk to them about something serious that deeply affects you. Let them know you're confiding in them because he or she has always proven trustworthy. This could be very beneficial to your well being. They may even be able to help just by listening. Having someone who won't tell your secrets is valuable.

19. Pray to the Creator For The Strength To Not Let it Bother You.

Probably nothing in life is worse than having a seemingly unsolvable mental problem and feeling acutely aware of it at all times. Especially if you feel it's something cosmetically questionable, physically challenged, or just essentially wrong. It can eat you inside like the worst cancer! And there is no cure for it. Few would beg to differ.

But there are many who experience all kind of hardships. And when they know they are incapable of dealing with it themselves they seek the ultimate help that is beyond human comprehension... they ask help from the Creator. They ask Him to please allow them to put their problem in His hands, or for Him to give them the strength to lessen the problems on their minds, so they can go ahead with life's daily duties and routines.

Trying to deal with mental and physical problems is hard enough. And don't forget, it's hard on your loved ones too.

Because when you're showing dampened moods and spirits, they feel down too. Communication could be very difficult until finally the loved one asks you, *"What's wrong?"* Or, *"You sure have seemed down lately."* How are you going to respond? If you do, it most likely won't be the truth. Because, how can you tell someone about a problem like this? It's way too embarrassing! And when a problem is of this magnitude, there is little or nothing they can do about it anyway. Most of them probably aren't experiencing it themselves, or don't know anyone with that kind of insecurity, at least not that was revealed to them.

These kinds of problems are only resolved by attaining peace with yourself. Since many of us find it extremely difficult to reach this inner peace, we must seek the Higher Source, the Creator. This may mean verbally expressing your hardship to Him. But patience must be exercised, because finding inner peace could take months, years, or even a lifetime trying to achieve. It is not at all uncommon to hear an elderly person confess, "I am finally at peace with myself."

But why not work to attain this peace sooner rather than later? It will have a positive effect on your relationship with yourself and your overall quality of life.

20. Don't Think You Were Created To Be Gay.

In these modern times there have been so many explicit ideas, vague thoughts, various views, beliefs and opinions at the notion that *'some of us were created to be gay'*. Who comes up with these sayings? Are they really true? Does it really matter? And just how do they affect the majority of us men with small penises, who know beyond a shadow of doubt that we are not gay, yet periodically throughout our lives bout with ourselves concerning these self-imagined questions?

Thing is, some of us who suffer from these concerns, solely because of having a little penis, also tend to experience decreases in self-esteem about our entire package, especially our manhood and masculinity. And just to further remove all doubt, we begin hopelessly searching for any mental and physical signs (that could be viewed by others) as having femininity. And so what if we found some... Relax, gentlemen. This isn't conclusive of anything.

The problem is, we gentlemen can't relax about anything, especially if it's about penis size. And the gay community is anything but ready to relax when it comes to talking about penis size. They relentlessly pursue the subject faster than hand conversation with broke wrist! Gay guys love a man and his penis. They seem to adore a dick, just short of worship. And they aren't afraid to talk about it. Many times in their conversations, talking about somebody else's dick is the center of attention! They give dick the power. And overtones of penis envy circulate the air. In an animated gay community world, I could see a giant penis erected on Center Street, like the Washington Monument, with all the gay community residents gravitating towards it and ejaculating it, I mean *'encirculating' it*, like moons and planets orbiting the sun. And when it comes to penis talk with verbal show & tell, those silly gossiping girls got nothing on the gay guys. Especially if they're sitting down, lower back arched, legs crossed with both hands atop one knee.

Okay, you're right, I got a little off the subject... I'm just saying, if your penis is too small, don't think you were created to be gay. Because in their world (generally speaking), just as with women, less than 4 inches erect is a complete turn-off. On one hand, men can't seem to get the visual satisfaction... and the social dissatisfaction soon follows. But on the other hand, some gladly write-off the visual in exchange for more suitable comfort and pleasure in their anus. Women, on the other hand, wouldn't just be turned-off, but annoyed as well. Claiming less than 4 inches erect visually couldn't get their juices flowing for sexual satisfaction, not to mention inability to hit the right spots.

One guy I knew was so distraught over having too small a penis, he said he never had sex. He said he was too embarrassed for any man or woman to see it, so he remained a virgin. He said that if a woman knew he was 2 inches soft and only 4 erect, he'd be the butt of all jokes with her friends. So he contemplated himself as being created to be gay. He figured his size could in no way pleasure a woman but could a man. Problem was he was not attracted to men. Therefore, he vowed to remain a virgin until the advent of a proven safe penis enlargement procedure. I can somewhat identify with that guy because in my first sexual experience not only did I cum in two seconds but I couldn't feel any pussy resistance what-so-ever. She lay there 30 minutes waiting for me to get it back up, but I couldn't. Then she told me, *"Maybe sex isn't for you"*... That statement bothered me for years. And I asked myself was I created to be gay, just because I couldn't feel any resistance? And just because of my embarrassment, we never had sex again. I just had to make myself believe that she was just some big pussy tramp that I had to get over and move on... me and my little dick...

The Gift of Gay Presence and Influence Today

Start this subject and I'm afraid it won't finish. Penis envy, perspective, flamboyance, intelligence, confidence, expression. Pick one. Where do we start? Doesn't matter, 'cause gay people can move it all. Just look at how society is moved by them; and how they have moved society to their liking, to seek their presence and how they do it.

They have changed the game with 'attention' being the focus. Anybody can get attention, but everyone can't command it. Many of us are attention seekers. (Some of us are 'attention whores'.) But they are attention-getters. And people pay for it. Just reflect on the media industry. They have done an 'about face' on implementing gays with some form flamboyance to the screen. Gay roles played on TV continue to intrigue the interest of the viewers by charming them with out-spoken humor and flirting advances. It keeps the show alive without boredom, and no reason to channel surf. Media industries know this all too well. They use those characters to captivate our attention hopefully throughout the commercial breaks.

'Out Of the Closet'... we like that shit. Nah, we actually love it. And it's envied more on a personal level. Even without flamboyance because that self-acceptance shows bravery and balls. But it's what follows soon after that gravitates us toward openly gay people; and that is lack of inhibition, with a non-give-a-fuck attitude. That inhibition allows the 'in' to come the fuck *out*! Get *out*, and be *out*, already. It allows you to be you, and do you, with courageous intention. Wow, lack of inhibitions and courage. In that combination alone lies true strength. I wish I had that...

Something else I've always admired in openly gay people; charming social ability and people skills. My envy grows whenever I observe someone exercising great people skills. I mean, it's got to be the most noble ingredient in the con game, and the art of persuasion. Think about it... their personality alone can buy friends and attention faster than money ever could. And make you smile while buying it. Many of them are very intelligent. They specialize in backyard counseling, psychology and everyday relationships. They know people. They know people many people wish to know. And many people know of them that they themselves don't know.

Why do you think this is? Because good news and good service travels fast. Let's look at a place where good service is rendered, news is reported, created and upgraded about every five minutes; the beauty salon with the gay hair stylist. You know, that place where *dem hairdos gets did.* Where appointments don't mean much, 'cause you gotta wait anyway; and walk-ins don't expect speedy service but know they'll be entertained during the entire time their waiting. This is where it all goes down. Countless verbiage of pointless gossip, *'he said-she said'*, empty advice, and the never settling issue of male-female relationships. This is where the stage is set. Where a little *flambam* goes a long way. Where the gay guy has control, regulates traffic, and has the floor.

Women rush to the hair salon on a regular basis for more than just a hairdo from a good stylist who happens to be gay. They're going because they know they're in for a raw performance with good laughs and great conversation from a man who's not trying to fuck them. They're going because he empathizes with women, shows respect for women, and gives women uplifting advice. For women this is not just free counseling, this shit is therapy.

All in all, I give gay men the credit for daring freedom of expression. Uninhibited and the balls to express it! That's freedom there... Dat ain't easy... I don't have it. Most of us appear to be cowards held back by society, afraid to release, vent and express. Seems like if we had the balls to be free, we'd be better people and not so damned stressed out. I often hear gay guys ask me, *"Why you look so stressed out? Come over here and talk to me... Don't you let life stress you out like that... Look at me... Getting' all these grays in your hair 'n stuff..."*

Penis envy... yeah, I think gay people are the kings of penis envy. But I think we are the kings of *balls envy...*

PART III:

THERE IS A SHORT SIDE
(YEAH, WE KNOW)
BUT ALSO A BRIGHT SIDE

21. Relax… There Are Some Women Out There With Whom You Can Fill Up All Four Walls And Even Hit The Bottom.

You may have heard the saying: *'all pussy is good pussy'*. Well, that may be so, in its own right. But for countless thousands of men around the world with penises smaller than average, this popular notion couldn't be further from the truth! Pussies are like women; they come in all shapes and sizes. Also, different pussies look different, smell different and feel different.

They feel different because all pussies have different textures of vaginal skin unique to each particular woman. And the patterned surfaces of the vaginal walls to each individual pussy are uniquely different, thus feeling different. Also, the amount of vaginal secretion released by each vagina varies widely.

Consider past experience and future awareness, combine these with friction during sexual intercourse and you will soon understand what's being implied – some vaginas are so big and loose one would think she recently had a baby, or she's been dating male studs, while others run so deep you'd think it had a bottomless pit! Anyway you slice it, it seems the deck is always stacked against the man with the little dick, because rarely does he hear about or run into a woman with a little tight pussy tailor-made for a small penis.

These on-going odds could be a major source of frustration for him. But what he shouldn't do is try to discern the size of a woman's vagina by studying her anatomical parts. Just because a woman has a big derriere, wide hips or is well-endowed with large breasts doesn't by any means imply she has a big vagina to go with it. Likewise because a woman is skinny or petite doesn't necessarily mean she has a tight little pussy also.

But there are many women out there (who are not virgins)

that have smaller vaginas and are looking for a man who's not so well-endowed. To find them, one should go to places where promiscuity is discouraged – like religious centers. Or seek unions with women whom haven't had many sex partners. Or women of high morals who got married as virgins, and who haven't been married more than twice.

These women are less likely to have sex as frequently as others. Therefore, their vaginas will be firmer, tighter, and less likely to be loose and stretched outta shape.

If you can't find one this way, seek a woman who works out often. Reason being, while flexing and contracting other bodily muscles, the vaginal muscles get worked also, giving her the ability to better contract her vagina and make it smaller and tighter.

22. Relax… Having A Small Penis Doesn't Mean You're Less Fertile Or A Prime Candidate For Impotency.

Believe it or not, for some unknown reason, many men who have small penises arrive at the absurd conclusion that having less length and girth also means they're less fertile than men with large penises. Not only that, they tend to think they will suffer from impotence at an earlier age. To attribute these as downfalls or characteristics of having a little penis is medically unfounded and without scientific logic.

Nonetheless, it is assumed by some that because a large penis enters, penetrates and fills up a vagina to a greater extent that the sperm are indeed closer to the egg, making it so the sperm require less endurance for the ultimate swim and are therefore stronger and more fertile.

Zinc deficiency has been linked to infertility and low testosterone levels. If you are currently engaging in intense workouts (especially cardiovascular), make sure to step up your zinc levels by eating more oysters, wheat germ, and fortified breakfast cereals. In conjunction with a vegetarian diet, athletic training and /or rigorous exercise can deplete your body of the zinc it needs to repair cells and grow new ones.

As far as sexual impotency goes – it is basically an inability to have an erection and has nothing to do with penis size. But if impotency is your only worry, then I suggest you quit smoking immediately, as it's been proven to cause impotency.

Sexual impotence and infertility are separate issues – totally unrelated to penis size!

23. Relish The Fact That Many Women Complain That A Big Penis Hurts Too Much.

One very effective way a man with a little penis complex can get some mental and emotional relief is by realizing and accepting the fact that many women complain that a large penis hurts too much. And these women's complaints and displeasures aren't to be taken lightly. But slightly to the contrary – it's not just a big penis alone that hurts a woman's vagina during intercourse. It's more so the man's insensitivity, his clumsiness and inconsideration, coupled with a large penis that does most of the harm. And men with small penises can take enjoyment in the fact that most of these women will always feel this way.

Women charge that his big penis, along with society's public excitement over it, have contributed to his ego, his sexual impatience and overly aggressive nature during intercourse. They further complain that when this type of man gets an erection, his advances are too quick and inconsiderate, and result in little more than pounding the pussy – regardless of her lack of sexual arousal and vaginal readiness. Instead of just trying to plunge and pound the hell out of her pussy, men with larger penises should realize they pose a hurtful problem for their mates, simply by not being patient enough to get her sufficiently aroused first through extended foreplay.

Generally speaking, most vaginas are capable of handling a larger penis. But they must be adequately lubricated before a large penis can enter without harm. Still in all, some women, regardless of how aroused they become, are intimidated by a large penis.

Others are afraid to have sex with men with large penises because they tend to behave clumsy and insensitively arrogant. For example, just before actual penetration he attempts to enter her vagina, but due to his larger size hits an entrance of resistance, and because of his impatience has doubts whether he's contacting the vagina, therefore he begins poking around, hitting her anus and the area between the anus and vagina, annoying her, and making her feel uneasy.

But by far what women hate most about a man with a big penis is one who behaves insensitively rough with it. The man who delights and takes pleasure in hammering a woman's pussy until she screams from true pain, and cries with helpless tears. And even if the sexual intercourse is going great, if she climaxes with an orgasm, loses her arousal and vaginal wetness, and he continues to thrust his penis inside of her, he could seriously harm her and even cause her vagina to bleed. At the very least, he could irreversibly damage her emotions.

Some women say no, or are reluctant to have sex with a man who's well-endowed because she fears he can't be gentle – imagining that the whole ordeal will be unpleasant and painful.

The typical sexuality and attitude of a man who has a large penis is often overbearing and haughty. He looks to himself as a cherished gift to women, and his penis as a prized tool every woman wants. He thinks all women fantasize about a penis like his, and would love to have sex with him anytime, at any given moment. And he swears and truly believes that women love for him to continually pound on their pussies until they cry. But this is not true, and most women HATE IT. Nor will they ever give him a second chance... reason being, he took too much pleasure out of hurting her.

24. Relish The Fact That Many Women Don't Want To Get Stretched Outta Shape.

For the most part, everybody loves and enjoys having sex. From childhood we are taught and informed about the up-and-coming intimate event. We are constantly primed for sex as we get bombarded by titillating images and erotic content, such as billboard advertisements, magazines, television and discussions with friends.

By far the most prominent role is played by peer pressure. From the start, boys and girls are taught differently (especially in America) about moral standards, conduct and societal judgments about having sex. Among them, boys are taught that women are sexual conquests, a sort of target practice. That their degree of studly-ness is only defined by the amount of different women they can sleep with, which entitles them to a badge of honor for their sexual prowess.

On the flipside of sexual education, women are taught quite the contrary. They're told not to be sexually promiscuous and to be faithful to one man at a time. And if they become sexually loose and unrestrained they will immediately be labeled *easy, cheap, slut* and *whore*. Along with this label comes the understanding (real or imagined) that her vagina is loose and stretched outta shape, which earns her a badge of dishonor and shame.

There are other reasons why women don't want their vaginas stretched outta shape. One reason is that they often hear that men detest it and hate it with a passion! Not necessarily because the man feels or knows she's been sleeping around, but rather during the sex act he feels little or no friction at all. Therefore he will quickly get rid of her and find someone he's more fitting with; one whose vagina doesn't question or challenge his manhood.

Women know that some men think of them as nothing more than sex objects, and other than sex, there's no relationship. Even more troubling is that some women feel their entire worth is built around sex, and other than that there's very little they can offer a man. These are narrow, nonetheless, true feelings people have of one another.

Men with small-penis insecurity must realize that women want men to desire them throughout their lives. And they want a man to lay claim to them – to keep them steadily. Women know the majority of a man's ego and his maleness comes from his penis (and the size of it, in some cases) and therefore his manhood must always be intact and constantly supported – even if the only support comes by wet fleshy vaginal skin tightly enclosed around his penis.

25. Relish The Fact That Only A Small Percentage Have Large Penises.

If you asked a great number of men around the world the question: *"If you could have 3 wishes that would change anything about yourself, what would they be?"* And then demanded their answers right on the spot, their answers would more than likely be:

"I'd like to be a few inches taller."

"I'd like to have a rock-hard muscular physique."

"I'd like a higher paying job."

These are just some of the more common and general responses the average guy would give to a complete stranger conducting a survey.

But on the flip-side, if you were to conduct the same survey but instead of demanding the answers right then and there, told the men to take their time (whether a few hours or days) and that their answers would be totally confidential on a small piece of paper, and only turned over to the "Wish Maker" himself, almost always one of their most secret dreams and desires would reveal, *"I wish I had a bigger penis."*

This penis secret is true, and very typical of men everywhere. But for the man who sincerely believes his penis is too little, this subject is very touchy and most delicate, and could be volatile to his emotions. This is a subject he would love to hear discussed, but at the same time hates to discuss, yet wants to discuss it. He hates to discuss it because he swears everybody has a bigger penis than his. And it angers and upsets him to hear his buddy saying his woman screamed and loved it all the while he kept ramming her with his big dick.

Word of comfort is, though, most men do not have a big dick. It is only a small percentage of men who are well-endowed with a large penis. Only a small percentage... So take delight in this fact!

Another thing men with small-penis complexes need to work on is their jealousy of other men that they believe got it goin' on a little more in the size department. If these insecure individuals see or know another man with a much larger penis than theirs, they covet his natural endowment with a passion, and tend to harbor envy towards him, even though it is his best friend.

In many cultures and societies, popular notions have it that if a man has a big nose, big hands or big feet, it also means he has a big dick too. Not true! Just another myth... all it means is just that - he has a big nose, big hands or big feet!

But the most damaging and unrealistic myth men throughout the world hold, is the unsubstantiated belief that the bigger a man's penis, the better he'll be able to make the woman feel, and the more satisfied she'll be.

But why do they continue to think this, when most of them have seen girls run away from guys whom the girls know of, or heard of, as having a huge dick? Most girls act scared, and for good reason. Hell, they don't want to get hurt! And they swear without a doubt he'll try and do just that – hurt 'em! But to quell most women's fears (and especially yours); the vagina is also known as the *great accommodator* that has the ability to expand or contract to the penis size that enters it. So there, you don't have to worry as much that he's giving her more feeling and pleasure than you're giving her. Because the size of the penis has almost nothing to do with the amount of pleasure the woman receives.

Just a few general facts about penis size, though. When measured from pubic bone to the tip of the head, average penis sizes range from 2.8 to 5.5 inches long. But when the penis is in full erection their size range grows smaller. And proportionally speaking, surprisingly, a smaller penis grows and swells more than a large penis during erection. In many cases, it is not uncommon to find a man's limp penis size more than double in size when erect (that is, in cases of men with smaller penises). But the average length of full erections is usually 5 to 7 inches. Measurements in girth (width) vary similarly...

All these facts, along with reasoning and the desire for self-help should at least rid the penis-insecure man of covetous envy or exaggerated jealousy of men naturally well-endowed. If not, at least relish the fact that only a small percentage of men the world over have penises much larger than the average.

PART IV:

TALK TO WOMEN ABOUT IT... BUT ONLY IN "THIRD" PERSON

26. Ask Women: "Does Size Really Matter?"

This suggestion is more geared to the small penis-insecure man who, no matter what is said positive about his anatomy, his physical make-up or his beautiful personality, he still believes penis size is all that really matters.

He's hopelessly bent on this thought even though close buddies (with the same complex, or without the complex but with a small penis) constantly tell him that having a little dick *"don't mean nothing"*, and that their women are head-over-heels in love with them and will do anything for them – little dick and all.

Although he hears women of all adult ages declare strongly and publicly, even on TV talk shows, that the size of a man's penis doesn't really matter, he still believes penis size is everything.

Yet when it comes to his penis during sex, these women emphatically stress *"its how he uses it"* more so than the size of it. And surprisingly, they are also candid in their concern about his ability to sustain an erection. Over and over, these seem to be the two standards by which women judge a man's performance in bed, but that's only as far as the man's penis is concerned.

When a woman tells you that penis size doesn't really matter, you must realize that she's viewing the sex act from an entirely different perspective than yours. It's by no means purely physical to her, but also emotional. Unlike yours, a woman's nature instructs her to take in other considerations, like:

How thoughtful is he during sex?

Is he considerate of her particular needs during sex?

Does he cater to her desires during sex?

Does he express sensitivity to her emotional needs before and after sexual intercourse?

This is by far what women desire most during intimate sex. All these *side acts* working together at the appropriate time, including penetration, with a small or average penis, is what makes a woman look highly favorable towards that man.

But chances are you don't really believe me, or you think I may have a good point but just aren't convinced, yet. Well, if uncertainty is your response, I knew this also could be expected, that's why I posed the action: Ask Women: Does It Really Matter?

So venture abroad and take your own personal survey asking women, *"Does penis size really matter?"* And more often than not, just before answering, a woman's nature will instinctively consider other factors, overriding her reactive conscience and compelling her to answer: *"No, it doesn't really matter."*

27. Ask Women: "Could You Be Content With A Small Penis?"

Men who are overly self-conscious in a negative way about their small penises, to the point that they think women in no way possible could ever be satisfied year after year with a little penis, should prove this idea themselves by asking women: *"Could you be content with a small one?"*

Go anywhere around the world, interviewing women of different cultures, different backgrounds, different religions, and women from all different races, and you will find responses disproportionately favored toward *"Yes."*

Basic reason being, the masses of women or the average woman encounters, experiences, and settles down with a man equipped with an average-size penis. This being fact, one can assume that the bulk of these women are satisfied and content with the size of their mate's penis. As the saying goes; *"You can't miss what you never had"*.

And if these women are happy in regards to their mate's average penis size, then having an inch or two smaller would not make or break a sexual relationship, nor deprive the woman of sensual ecstasy. As a matter of fact, men with average-sized penises sometimes encounter women who during sexual intercourse complain that, *"it hurts too much, take it out!"*

And this is not because the woman is too dry or not releasing enough vaginal secretions. She's probably just built too small for his size, even though his size is only considered average. In this case, the woman would be delighted and totally content if her mate's penis was just a couple inches smaller in length, or smaller in girth, or maybe even both.

One other attestation to the fact that most women will be content with a man who has a small penis, is the way we've all seen how women react to the men on TV talk- shows who get dumped solely because the women who dumped them claim they were lousy lovers in bed. And if the man fires back at her lousy performance in an attempt to save face, the woman usually retaliates harder and even crueler by telling the national audience, *"He has a little penis!"*

Of course this accusation always invokes the loudest audience response. But the irony of it is, as long as the man appears to be a nice guy (which he usually does) there will always be a few women in the studio audience who will tell the show's host that they would love to date him (lousy lover, little dick and all!) And if he's good-looking, too, the show will receive tons of mail from women all over inquiring about dating that man!

So go figure... women will be content with a man who has a small penis because, to most women, penis size does not matter... provided he could improve on his lovemaking skills if need be. What ultimately matters to women is that the man be supportive of her, loving to her, kind to her, and faithful to her. Fulfill her desires in these areas and she'll swear you're the most precious lover she's ever had.

28. Ask Women: "Could A Vagina Accommodate A Small Penis?"

Although this title suggests asking women, *"Could a vagina accommodate a small penis?"* I will also give an opinion from a man's perspective and attempt to briefly explain why some men continue to have trouble grasping the idea that a vagina *will* accommodate a small penis.

Some men with small penises tend to perceive a women's vagina as a sort of rubber band-like tunnel. One that has a set standard size, but at any given time can increase in its width, depth and circumference, but at the same time could never decrease or contract from its set standard size, allowing it to accommodate a smaller penis.

Other men tend to harbor in their psyche deeply ingrained images of nude or scantily-clad women engaged in sexually explicit activities on-screen, off-screen, in advertisements and in adult magazines doing something sexually explicit. Images across the board ranging from women having sex with well-hung men or penetrating themselves with huge dildos, to images of female strippers bumping and grinding on a fire pole, sliding on it, caressing it – implying lewd sexual overtures. Insecure men cannot escape even subtler images, like a woman talking to a man while holding a banana, carrot or cucumber. Every image that reminds him and everything he sees associated sexually with a vagina is very big, much bigger than the average penis, not to mention a smaller-than-average penis.

With images like these coming to mind, one can easily understand how a penis-insecure man could wonder if a vagina could accommodate his small penis. And it's almost a miracle if he *doesn't* have a mental breakdown or acute sexual phobia.

One thing any man insecure about such images should understand, is that they are just that, images and nothing more. Of course, there are women out there who are built big enough to handle a huge dildo, etc. Still and all, most of these women who participate in pornography go home to men with average-sized penises. They don't do this full-time! What they're doing is earning their living by helping to create the images that sell the most, and are very attractive eye-catchers, that sexually entice.

They could very well do an image of a vagina accommodating a small penis (and they do), but it is not as visually stimulating, and doesn't sell as much. It must also be remembered and reflected on, that just as there are, and always will be, countless men who are not well-endowed but built rather small; there are, and always will be, countless women who are built rather small on the inside, thereby, allowing perfect harmony and a perfect accommodation between her and her mate.

29. Ask Women: "Is A Large Penis A Mere Visual Turn-on, Or Physical As Well?"

First it must be noted that the opinions, perceptions, and points of view on male and female genitalia seldom differ within the same gender. But, on the other hand, when the same questions on male and female genitalia are posed to both sexes, the perceptions and answers between the two almost always differ.

Surprisingly though, many answers from males tend to be subjective and rarely supported by any scientific study. Probably the main reason men so badly want to know from women whether a large penis is merely visual, or physical as well, is on account of men placing too much of their worth, too much of their value, and too much of their manhood on sexual performance and their penis size.

It naturally follows that, since men place all these eggs in one basket, they ultimately expect women to judge and grade them accordingly. Problem is, women simply don't have a one-track mind when it comes to sex and relating to a man. Women are a more emotional creation than men – they take in the full feelings of emotional and physical pleasure during the entire sexual experience; and are therefore virtually incapable of isolating a single aspect of the sex act.

But of course, I'm speaking largely in general; like most things, there are exceptions to the rule. Undoubtedly, there are a small percentage of women with whom a large penis is more erotically physical than anything... and is always preferred. Seemingly, these women would settle for nothing less. And if not given their choice, they would sometimes appear disappointed or not enthused before sex and during sex, and even after sex outwardly show their dissatisfaction whether verbally or by demeanor. Some of these women desire a large penis because they enjoy and get-off on hard and heavy strokes. They insist that it takes a large penis (mostly in girth) to trigger their *G-spot,* and add that since the G-spot is located on the roof inside the vagina a larger penis is more suited to make contact and stimulate that area.

Others like their pussies treated roughly, even battered with repeated pounding. Masochism seems to be the underlying cause, because the goal would appear to be a pussy used, abused and sorely mistreated.

Some women prefer a man with a big dick because it's more so a combination of the visual, physical and mental. They love the feeling of their vagina being filled-up and the idea of a long penis penetrating through their stomach, combined with the wild visual trip they go on from watching a huge dick take deep probing strokes in and out of their vagina.

Still, with other women, a large penis is merely visual, and a medium or small penis would do just fine. The thing about a large penis is that when clad in tight or thin contour-revealing clothes it has the power to excite and arouse a woman just as much as a man gets when he sees a woman's exposed big breasts and cleavage. But just as every man isn't turned on by a woman's big breasts; every woman isn't turned on by a man's big penis. To many people, big anatomy is real nice to look at and maybe even to touch (to overcome curiosity) but not to become sexually intimate with them. Even if a woman is turned on by the sight of a big penis; some of these same women still view such men as not normal... a freak of nature... a circus sideshow... or even a fantasy man – and what do most people do about their fantasies? Nothing. They allow them to stay just that – fantasies.

So ask women if a large penis is merely visually a turn-on, or physically as well, and you'll probably get some surprising answers. Some women prefer their man to have a big penis, not necessarily because they think it feels better, but because they view the man as more manly, and themselves as more feminine during sexual intercourse. Even though the man be gentle, the woman still feels not in control, conquered and subdued (like she wants to feel) because in the back of her mind she knows he has the potential to pound her pussy to submission or drive her to the hilt, whether in ecstasy or in pain.

Still, there will always be a sizable percentage of women who are loyal never to let their vagina come in contact with an over-sized penis, no matter how much they might like to *look* at them... because they are just built too damn small! ...Sounds wonderful, huh?

30. Ask Women: "Could A Small Penis Give You A Climax?"

Probably every woman who's been asked this question, or has even brought this question to mind, will generally come up with the quick answer, *"Yes"*. But in spite of this assured and consistent answer from women of all different types, men with small penises refuse to retire this question. It is a question men have allowed to perpetuate from media hype magnified by their own insecurities.

So as it goes, men will continue to forward this unsettling question, and women will keep responding with favorable answers, like: *"It's not the size of the penis that counts – but the way you work with what you've got."* Or, *"It ain't the size of the ship, it's the motion in the ocean."*

These responses from women are so common and so plentiful

that they must be taken as honest and sincere. Which is very fortunate for the man with the smaller penis, because now he can stop self-deteriorating his own mental and emotional state by worrying about his penis size and trying to please a woman through it.

Instead, he can now focus and concentrate on his technique. And with women, good technique out-measures penis size any day. A man having good technique during intercourse is so important to a woman that it holds the most influence in her heart when it comes to her personal *stamp of approval* on a man's sexual performance.

Many times, a woman's idea of good technique and great performance in a man lie solely in his ability to maintain an erection. For many women, even if a man has a little penis and bad technique to boot, yet had above-average staying power, he would be considered a good sex partner. First, because a woman feels that he's fresh and inexperienced, therefore she can school him and mold him exclusively to her sexuality – and by chance get him pussy-whipped! Second, she feels that if he had poor technique but could sustain a hard-on long enough for her to get an orgasm, she could slow his movements to almost nothing; take over herself with movements good enough and erotic enough to satisfy them both, and then drive herself to climax! Once she's released her tension, if he still hasn't released his, she would allow him to do whatever he needs to reach ecstasy – little penis, bad technique and all!

And if by chance you suspect your technique needs improvement, then try something new and observe her response. Or, better yet, ask her to show you or guide you in another way she likes, then stick with that way for a good while. Whatever you do, don't ask her, *"Is my technique alright?"* Cause if it's not she'll be very unwilling to tell you. One technique that's effective with a small penis is to penetrate her, but instead of thrusting in and out rotate in a churning motion, round and round. This allows much better contact and stimulation with her clitoris, which alone could drive her to orgasm.

But to make a woman have an orgasm through penile penetration doesn't require any ingenuity in technique, and it doesn't take a big penis. In fact, a little penis will do just as well. All it takes is a lot of emotional love and affection, and some basic strokes. Reason being, the inner and outer lips of the vagina, the funnel-shaped area between the inner lips just above and outside the vaginal opening, and the first two inches of the vaginal entrance itself, (excluding the clitoris) are the most sensuous and sensitive areas on a female's pussy, because all are richly supplied with nerve endings, making them extremely sensitive to penetration, no matter what the size. And just to make matters better for the *"little"* man, the deep inner walls of the vagina, (where a large penis would also make contact), are rather numb by comparison.

So if your woman doesn't climax, don't blame it on your small penis, it's probably something your woman is doing or not doing, or is incapable of doing at the time –or perhaps the foreplay didn't get her ready enough.

Oh, and one more thing... female relationship experts and female sex therapists discount the factor and affects of a large penis as compared to a smaller one half its size during sexual intercourse – don't you watch the talk shows?

PART V:

HOW TO DRESS A SMALL PENIS

31. Don't Wear Tight Pants.

If you're overly self-conscious about your small penis size or have a serious "little dick" complex, then wearing tight pants is probably not for you. More often than not, when people dress in tight clothing they do it with the sole intention of revealing the outline of their body contour. When men wear tight pants they often check during the day to see if the shape of their penis is showing or not.

And when men who are self-conscious in this way see other men wearing tight pants they for some reason or another (usually insecurity), feel compelled to look at the other men below their belts, just to see if they can discern penis size.

But this need-to-see inclination without a doubt will prove to be damaging to his self-esteem. It's just the law of averages: keep looking' for the Big One, and time and time again you'll find it. And when you do, a mounting self-pity will be the only result.

32. Wear Boxer-Type Underwear Instead Of Briefs.

Although, briefs are obviously sexier to some women than boxer-type underwear, there are a significant amount of ladies who swear by boxers. And most women definitely support the notion that boxers are the more masculine!

Boxers allow a man's genitals to exist in their natural state... unrestricted. Unlike the over-support, constriction and slight compression that briefs impose on the male genitalia of small stature, boxers allow the liberty of free movement, and the penis and testicles to 'hang' in their intended state. This 'hang' (thanks to gravity) forces the penis into a more elongated position; therefore, the penis and testicles look bigger.

Furthermore, on a health note, medical reports suggest that

wearing tight pants and briefs can contribute to infertility in men.

33. Don't Hang Out In Cold Weather.

Just like us, our body parts loathe being exposed to cold climates. Hands, feet, nose, lips and ears can even suffer frostbite. At the minimum, overexposure to intense cold leaves our body parts numb, with a slight feeling of pain when bumped or squeezed, making our only desire at this time to withdraw them into heat-hoarding fabrics.

But men with small penises have one more thing to fear when hangin' out in cold weather... shrinkage! First of all, there is no 'hang', which is mentally devastating in itself. Second of all, as if the first wasn't bad enough, this little penis (especially in cold weather) seems to have a brain of its own. The more cold it senses, the further it retracts, pulling itself back within itself, resembling folds of skin, like bellows.

Sometimes the penis withdraws so far that it's about half the size of a Vienna sausage! This shrinkage phase is very agitating because the head of the penis is facing horizontal and not pointing downward. At this position it is extremely uncomfortable because the penis head is constantly rubbing against the pants causing major discomfort to an already sensitive area, especially when wearing denim. So take my advice and keep your penis warm.

34. Don't Wear Tight Pants Or Biker Shorts To The Gym Or In Public.

If having a small penis makes you feel less manly or just embarrasses the hell outta you, the last thing you want to do is involuntarily show it off or give others a direct viewing target of it.

Well, that's exactly what biker shorts and dolphin-type shorts do; they are made to highly accentuate one's anatomy by clinging close or tightly to the body parts, contouring all shapes, lines, and curves.

You might argue that only biker shorts do that and not dolphin shorts, necessarily, because they fit sort of loosely. Well, because of the thin material they're made from, they easily lay on things, kinda taking on their shapes, but leaving a clear imprint of what lies beneath. And in light of a little penis (lets say, one of size where the head points horizontal or the shaft isn't long enough for the head to turn the curve and point downward) the material shows it as some *'little thing-ee'* (like a marble) poking or protruding out. These types of shorts are definitely a gym attire *'don't'*. I know, you're just trying to show off a great pair of legs, but at the same time, the women are looking for that *third* leg. You can best believe the woman working out next to you is going to zero-in on that 'marble' and think to herself, *"What the hell is that little thingee? That better not be his dick!"*

And, hey Buddy! What are you tryin' to do here anyway? Make reality of the myth that all buff men have small penises? C'mon man, we're still fightin' to keep that statement general.

But even with all the drawbacks dolphin-type shorts have, the popular biker-type shorts will probably get even more attention. And so will that marble look-alike contest you'll be performing while wearing 'em. Biker shorts not only make it clear to others whether or not you're hangin' a Polish sausage or a Vienna sausage, they can also accentuate a couple of other sexual features that could no doubt excite the right woman's fetish: a man's balls... and of course, his butt!

For some women, just seeing a clear imprint of a man's balls bulging out of his clothes is turn-on enough. But for many others, the greatest sexual feature on a man is his butt – that is, if he has a great one, of course. So before you dare throw on that pair of bikers throw in a few sets of glute squeezers. Because even if you did place 1st in that marble look-alike contest, at the least your sexy backside could focus her attention away from your front side. Oh yeah... just what kind of a marble are you 'fronting' anyway; a shamrock, a crystal, or a cat-eye? If you're gonna play marbles you'd better be using a *boulder!*

35. *Wear Tight Pants Or Biker Shorts To The Gym Or In Public.*

Seems like a contradiction to some of the previous suggestions? Well, not really… bear with me.

Way back when, the gym use to be a place built on exercising, getting fit, and not much else. But all that's changed! Although, they still exercise to get in shape, more and more people frequent gyms and health clubs with the intention of showing off their physiques, especially the details of the curvature, size and shape of their anatomy. Let's face it, gyms have turned into a human meat market, a kind of sexually alluring social scene for young and old alike.

Many men with small penises love to go to co-ed health clubs to workout. And some of them desire nothing more than to have a sexual relationship with one of the scantily-clad women they find there. But they're often hesitant to approach because in the back of their minds they swear (whether true or not) she has been fantasizing about the man on the next machine with the Chiquita banana exposing itself in his crotch area.

This topic is addressed to the man who feels he can't compete with the guy with the huge prick on display. So in order for him to feel comfortable about a sexual relationship with one of these women, he must first be assured that she is comfortable with his penis size. Therefore, he lays it all on the line by wearing tight biker shorts or sweats, leaving no mystery for her to uncover. This way, he knows that she sees it and can either love it or leave it! YOU GO, BOY!

36. Don't Often Parade Freely Around The House In Sexy Tight Briefs If You're In An Unstable Relationship.

To often walk around the house in sexy brief-type underwear is cool, sometimes – especially if you've got a sexy physique to flaunt. But sexy underwear to a man may not be sexy underwear to a woman – especially when it comes to tight-fitting briefs. Thing is, many women don't think tight butt-hugging panty-type briefs for men are sexy at all – but rather sissy-like. And if you don't have a sexy body to go along with those panties, her thoughts might not differ. But even worse, if you don't have a big dick to compliment those tight briefs it might piss her off.

Some women will think you're competing with them, because they want the sole role of prancing around in tight panties. Women get enough competition from other women; they don't want it from their man. So if you're gonna do it, you'd better have a nice body or a big dick to keep her thoughts in check.

And fellahs, this is a complete *'no-no'* if your relationship is in trouble and you've got a little dick. NEVER allow her to buy you, help you pick out, or even see you looking around trying to pick out a pair of underwear. If you've seen the photos of the guys modeling briefs on the front of the packages, you know exactly what I'm talking about. All the models either have big dicks bulging out the front of the briefs, or are wearing some type of implant to make it appear like they are well-endowed. Anyway, the women see these photos and they say, *"Wow"* and ogle at those big penises.

And then picture you or see you in 'em and get pissed the fuck off! No longer will she view you as wearing sexy tight underwear, but as a little-dick man with panties on.

Ever notice that she never gives you compliments when you wear them? Probably because she doesn't think it's manly, or because you pissed her off for wearing 'em without the prize inside. A point to ponder: if she's thinking about leaving you because the sex isn't great, then hey, you don't want to give her any visible encouragement.

PART VI:

EXERCISE THAT SMALL PENIS

37. Do 'Penis' Cardiovascular Exercise.

Studies show that men who think negatively about their small penis size consequently develop other negative opinions of self-hate and dislike. This can contribute to an apathetic mental state, frequent bingeing on unhealthy food, gaining unwanted pounds, and showing non-interest and a poor outlook on life.

One way to definitely change this tide is to do exercise – especially cardiovascular exercise. Cardiovascular exercise is the branch of exercise that involves and directly affects and conditions the heart, the blood, the blood vessels and the lungs as a unified body system. Cardiovascular exercise is also a training activity which enables one to strengthen and develop particular muscles as well as the body and the mind overall by some systematic practice exerting the body, like brisk walking, running, swimming, dancing, and roller-blading. Cardiovascular exercise not only combats unwanted weight gain and low self-esteem, but working out regularly gives you a healthy, better-looking body. And when you (and especially others) notice this change it will also change the way you see yourself and everything around you!

A healthy lifestyle that includes cardiovascular exercise builds self-confidence and self-esteem. With this new confidence and esteem comes improved concentration and creativity. And if either of these are in effect, one will no doubt experience a reduction in stress and worry, which in turn leaves one more relaxed.

For the man who suffers from an emotional problem such as a small-penis complex, just being less stressed and more relaxed could greatly contribute to an acceptance of himself for who he is and what he has been given.

Just remember; in order to have an active sex life and the strength to do so, one must work toward a healthy mind and a youthful disposition about life. Because mind and body are intimately connected, exercise is the perfect medium. Therefore, one must devise an exercise program to keep himself healthy. For starters, a new workout program shouldn't be for more than forty-five minutes each session, four days a week. And as far as targeting the penis muscle directly, hey, just get in the shower, drape that wet towel across your dick and *flex, release... flex, release...* and don't forget to breath...

38. Work Out – Get Buffed!

In high school, we all heard the stigmas and stereotypes associated with muscle-bound buff guys – they're big and clumsy... and there's the popular saying: *"You either got a little brain or a little dick!"* This stereotype has lingered for decades, and was largely responsible for keeping many a man with a small-penis complex out of the gym. Whether this reputation ever had true validity, the notion has fast begun to wane. And mature women just don't seem to care about it much. They are more concerned with an overall picture of good health.

And nothing is more beautiful and says *'good health'* like a well-defined, muscle-toned body. Men with small penises appreciate this change of heart. The results are apparent in the Speedo 'fillings' at gyms and fitness clubs: you see more Vienna Sausages than you do Wieners and Bananas!

When insecure men begin developing their physiques nicely, they gain more self-esteem and start posing in mirrors and strutting about with confidence – but not with excessive pride and arrogance. Reason being, in their heart of hearts they still feel emotionally insecure and physically inadequate; which serves as a reminder and grounds them in humility. But his muscular body along with a humble attitude and modest behavior is a quality package much desired by women.

A woman has always been attracted to a man who appears to care much about his health. But a masculine body with packed-on muscle, women regard as an added sensual bonus! For when she presses her warm soft figure against his masculine hard body her nature immediately brings out her femininity, compelling her preoccupation with sensual lusts and carnal desires. A woman gets so turned on by a man with muscles, that ordinary sex becomes transformed into something more than just the emotional and physical love she has for him. She will soon realize that sex with her muscle man is a source of thrills and excitement. Sex becomes her ultimate expression of intimacy. And since women love to cuddle, snuggle, and be caressed, she will often initiate intimacy with clear sexual gestures just as an excuse to fondle his body, get close and press skin. For her, just looking at your buffed hard body or even thinkin' about it (even clothed) will act as a mild aphrodisiac!

This is one of the rare times a woman will step into the physical realm and allow herself to become a visual creature (like the male is ninety percent of the time). And how could she not become visual and crave physical intimacy if her man possesses a great body with masculine broad shoulders, a massive rock-hard chest, lean rippling abdominals, a powerful-looking back like a cobra, and sexy big legs cut-up like a track star?

Attain a body that just looks half as good as that sounds, along with a loving attitude towards her, and she'll swear you're God's gift to her. She'll love you forever and won't find any fault with you – not even what you perceive as a small penis. Believe me, if she stays with you long enough for you to develop a nice body, then she probably never tripped on your little penis anyway.

Once your muscles start shaping up she's going to notice your self-esteem shooting through the roof. So be very careful... 'cause although you're still telling her you love her, she might think the new you, with all this attention and self-esteem is a bit much; and soon began to feel insecure that you're too good for her, or worse, that she's not good enough for you. Just remember to stay sensitive and considerate, and you won't have to worry about her feeling that way.

Anyway, to start your journey to a great body, first you must commit to an exercise program, perhaps with the help of a trainer that suits your body's intensity level. Slightly varying the routine from time to time will help keep it interesting and keep you motivated. Mainly though, concentrate on incline bench presses for upper chest, military press and side laterals for shoulders, bent-over rows and pull-ups for back, barbell bicep curls and tricep extensions for arms, and for legs, do squats.

39. Maintain A Flat Lean Stomach - Exercise Your Abdominals.

Just what does having a flat lean stomach do for a man with a small penis? Well…it gives him sex appeal – you know, that physical attractiveness and erotic charm that allure members of the opposite sex. Countless women attest to the idea that there's nothing that qualifies a man's sexuality like a hard, lean, ripped washboard stomach!

Case in point: during the precursory ritual of intimate foreplay, a woman can't resist the temptation of keeping one hand on a man's shapely, sexy mid-section. And if she ever attempts to perform fellatio, you can almost guarantee that just before her indulgence she'll rub, smooth-over and kiss your sculptured abs. Totally taken away by your sexy stomach, she'll forget all about your smaller penis size. Important not only it is to *attain* a flat stomach, but it is more important to *maintain* a flat stomach. Reason being, *'the look'* bespeaks much about an individual's persona, such as their self-worth, self-image, self-identity, and self-consciousness. It also shows that one chooses to eat to live, rather than live to eat.

When you constantly overeat and don't exercise to the point your gut and butt protrudes and your hips and waist spread, it creates a false illusion that the penis is smaller than it really is because the areas carrying extra weight are highlighted. Well, when you slim your tummy and taper your waist, your penis is highlighted instead.

One simple way to help keep you slim is walking – brisk walking, that is. Most people walk, of course, but most don't know that by increasing their speed and using a little more arm motion, walking becomes one of the best exercises known. When done properly, brisk walking is an excellent overall workout. Jogging in moderation can be added for those who need a little more intensity.

40. Eat Nutritious Healthy Foods.

Okay, I know. The first thought that comes to your mind is: *"How in the hell is eating healthy nutritious foods gonna make my dick any bigger?"*

Well, good news and bad news – it can't, but eating healthy can improve the frequency of your erections, *and* make them harder. This is achieved by clean unpolluted and unrestricted blood flow from the heart to the penis.

The heart pumps blood through three types of vessels. These blood vessels are called arteries, veins, and capillaries. The arteries transport the blood, which contains oxygen and nutrients (from our food) to the cells in the body. Arteries break off into very small blood vessels called capillaries. The heart and the body directly affect each other. This is why it is important to have clean unpolluted blood. For polluted blood is the cause of artery problems and it can most certainly adversely affect many of the body's organs, including the penis.

The consumption of meat and animal products is a huge cause for pollution of the blood. Especially meat. Meats pollute the blood by adding cholesterol at high levels. High cholesterol is a precursor to heart problems. Other foods and products that should be avoided or kept to a minimum are most dairy products, white flower products junk food, sugar, alcohol, drugs (legal & illegal) and cigarettes. When we eat animal products such as meats and dairy products, it's like adding waste to the body, and the blood cholesterol rises. Too much cholesterol in the blood results in atherosclerosis, which is the scarring, blockage, and weakening of the artery walls. This condition causes poor blood circulation to the penis, not to mention strokes and heart attacks.

Consumption of beef, pork, and white flour products thickens the blood, raises cholesterol and adds plaque build-up on the artery walls, resulting in less blood to the heart. This in turn means less blood to the penis. Less blood to the penis means less than full erections. But don't despair... less also means more... more sexual frustration, that is.

So, clean those walls by eating plenty of fruits and vegetables, white meat (chicken and turkey), and food that doesn't contain as much cholesterol, trans-fat, and white flour. Eating healthy will keep your artery walls clean, and your penis hard.

41. Develop 'Penis Control'.

For a man, having penis control is probably the best quality and the best weapon one could ever wish to have when it comes to sexual intercourse. When it all boils down, there's nothing in the world that a man wants more than to be able to please a woman. And there is absolutely, positively, no greater pleasure and no greater satisfaction than a man truly feeling that he has sexually and emotionally conquered the woman of his desires! And for most men, this mental and physical conquest comes by none other, than raw sex – hot and hard penetration.

But to accomplish this incredible feat requires time, and time demands *penis control*. Having penis control technically means having ejaculatory control. Having ejaculatory control basically means that a man is fairly able to control when he will ejaculate. He can stroke for a while to please him and her, but if she wants more for enjoyment or in order to climax, he's able to go much longer. Or he can be selfish – stroke it less than ten times and begin to ejaculate – it's up to him. This is real power!

Although they say sex is only 10% of a relationship, develop penis control and she will personally guarantee you got half the battle won! For she knows that developing the knack for penis control basically translates to a hard dick in her at all times… which might be the only raw talent in a man she ever cared about. Because to her, even stroking a few extra minutes is invaluable… and worth more than gold.

To be able to avoid premature ejaculation (other than the first round) is a mental and emotional victory for a man. But succumbing to it can be psychologically devastating. There are many ways to develop penis control, and everyone else's method may not work for you. But a practical way to start is to get in touch with your body – mainly the feelings of erotic sensitive stimulation. You're gonna have to become more conscious during sex – and you're gonna have to pay more attention to the details in feelings leading up to climax, during ejaculation and after ejaculation.

Practice on yourself first to find out exactly what it feels like as your sexual excitement ramps up to the plateau just before ejaculation. See if you can become conscious of when you hit that plateau and practice *penis control* to spend more time there before actually letting loose.

Learn to pace yourself during intercourse by stroking the vagina in intervals. You can still penetrate it but only stroke here and there. Take your time and don't rush. The goal is to delay ejaculation as along as possible, while still maintaining just enough sensual stimulation to keep a firm erection. Every time you began to feel the throbbing sensation that takes place moments before ejaculation, immediately stop thrusting until the feeling lessens, or even pull your penis out completely if it's feeling too good. Just rest a little. Play it off by acting like you're just trying to switch positions. But be mindful that she could get annoyed by you repeatedly pulling out too soon. And it's only too soon if she's in a groove and about to climax.

In between time fondle her. Play with her. Caress her. Whisper sweet nothings and come hither words in her ear – even talk dirty! Repeat these steps over and over until you gain some control over your ejaculation. Of course, you can figure out when it's time for you to *"go for what you know"*!

Breathing techniques can also be helpful in delaying ejaculation. But they are not as effective as the stop-and-go method and pacing yourself in intervals. During intercourse, concentrate on breathing in a slower steady rhythm, because rapid breathing and heavy panting can quickly urge on and arouse sensual feelings, making it easier for premature ejaculation to occur. Although, it can be very difficult while engaging in sexual intercourse, try inhaling for six seconds, then exhaling for six seconds for three straight minutes; when you succeed with that go for five... Breathing techniques take time to perfect, so exercise patience.

If everything else fails, think baseball... seriously, though. Taking your mind off the sex act and focusing it on something that has absolutely nothing to do with sex can be very effective. Remember... control the mind and the body will follow. To use the mental diversion technique you basically apply the same method – perform normally until you near the point of feeling an ejaculation coming – then distract your mind with boring politics, or even mumble under your breath all the President's names, and the dates they were in office. If this boring stuff doesn't make the sensual sensation go away, nothing will.

42. Stay Away From Sex Killers.

As if having a little dick wasn't bad enough! Using and abusing sex killers can severely dull your sex life – or wipe it out completely while using them. Some men with small penises feel there's nothing worse than having a little dick... but yes, there is... having a little dick that doesn't work is far worse!

Equally frustrating and emotionally devastating is only being able to achieve a partial erection. But that's what using sex killers can do to a man – dampen desire and inhibit erection. Major known sex killers are alcohol, tobacco, anti-depressants, illicit drugs and a bad diet.

Alcohol – ask just about anybody who's a drinker how alcohol effects their sex life and many would tell you that alcohol stimulated their sex life. Few would tell you that alcohol ruined their sex life. And some who are conscious of the number of drinks they have and are in tune with their body's reactions to each drink will tell you they only get sexually aroused up to two drinks, but any beyond that drowns their erection and/or inhibits performance.

Alcoholism wreaks havoc on the male reproductive system, reducing one's ability to produce normally formed sperm cells. This is because alcohol destroys the cells in the testes that manufacture testosterone, which will dull sexual desire, disrupt hormone levels, and sap sex drive. Then there's tobacco. Besides giving you yellow-stained teeth, bad breath and lung cancer (isn't that enough yet?), smoking also does wonders for the sex life – it impairs erection. Tobacco smoke does this by narrowing the blood vessels, impairing blood flow to the penis.

Antidepressants are drugs that alleviate the symptoms of depression. They work well for that, but not for sex. Antidepressants carry sexual side effects like loss of desire, impaired erections, difficulty reaching orgasm and conversely, premature ejaculation.

The latest antidepressants that have gained widespread popularity are selective serotonin reuptake inhibitors (SSRI's), sold under the name Prozac, Zoloft and Paxil. These also cause sexual side effects. But to relieve depression, yet cut the degree of side effects, lessen the dosage – either reduce to a of couple days throughout the week or the amount taken in a day (under a doctor's supervision).

Antihistamines are used to control allergic reactions and conditions, and are sold widely over-the-counter. They minimize or prevent the effects of histamine in the body. But they also impair sexual desire and sexual performance. Many also cause drowsiness that can dull desire on its own.

Illicit drugs are drugs that are prohibited, unauthorized, and not allowed by law. Downers, like tranquilizers and barbiturates can be dangerously addictive and have primary side effects of drowsiness and dizziness – two of which alone sap sexual desire and impair performance. Uppers like amphetamines, crystal-meth and cocaine stimulate sexual desire in some people, but are dangerously addictive with prolonged use and, inevitably, sexual desire fades as well.

PART VII:

PRACTICAL ADVICE FOR THE PENIS-INSECURE

43. Stop Looking At Pornographic Magazines!

Starting at a very young age throughout childhood, we boys learn quickly about the female body by snooping through piles of clothes in daddy's drawers and old boxes stashed away in the garage, and stumbling across girly magazines. Amazed at what we found, we'd spend day after day secretly sneaking off, outta fear of getting caught by our parents, just to gaze hesitantly, yet intently, at pictures of naked men and women.

Even though we saw photos of big long penises entering vaginas, our innocence persisted, and it never dawned on us to compare our size. As a matter of fact, we thought our own penis wasn't used for much more than taking a leak. Then we became sexually aware... and from then on to adulthood we men with small penises viewed pornography with a more personal purpose, and less intrigue: comparing the photographed dicks with our own became a major part in the objective.

But for men with 5 1/2 inches or less while fully erect, nothing came of it but feelings of inadequacy. These guys suffer other head-trips while peering in these magazines... such as seeing a close-up of a large penis totally filling a vagina. All the while decreasing his self-adequacy by imagining himself penetrating the same vagina, then realizing a full circular 360 degree slack between him and her. What do you think this does for his self-esteem? Men with small dicks must avoid these magazines! Because in many cases they leave the men feeling there's absolutely no way they can satisfy a woman sexually the way they most want to and the way women want them to.

Don't forget that the producers purposely scout out unusually large penises to feature in these pages.

44. Never Pay Too Much Attention To The Lyrics Of Some R&B and Hip-Hop Music.

If having a little penis affects you to the point where you feel uneasy about hearing people talk with enthusiasm about sex and their encounters, then listening too closely to the lyrics in some R&B and Hip-Hop music can surprisingly make you feel just as uneasy, or worse. If you find yourself listening mostly to this type of music, I strongly suggest you focus more so on going with the flow of the beat, and caution you against paying much attention to the lyrics.

As we all know, today's lyrics in many of these songs go unharnessed and are borderline censured. Songs overwhelmed with erotic phrases highly susceptible to sexual stimulation. Libido-arousing poems that leave no guesswork as to what's implied. And feelings of passion and desire expressed in sonnets, designated for erogenous zones. These lyrics are straightforward and in-your-face, rhapsodizing about specific areas of the body such as the genitals and breasts, and sexual activities, including oral and anal...

The male artists sing of their sexual prowess and total confidence in satisfying a woman, while female artists croon sentimentally and emotionally of a man fulfilling their feminine needs. Listening to these type songs over and over on the radio could sadden a sensitive man insecure about his sexual abilities, could lower his spirits, and sink him into immediate depression... even if just for the duration of the song.

45. Shorten Your Hours Of TV Watching!

It is commonly known that people who are burdened with mental, physical or social disorders tend to be more withdrawn because of them. Just like everyone else, they also seek solace. But people with emotional disorders often go one step beyond in seeking relief. As a result, they structure the major part of their lives around things that ease grief, loneliness, and stress.

Two prominent past-times of comfort are overeating and excessive TV watching. By indulging day after day in hours-on-end of TV without good purpose and for mere entertainment or escape, one involuntarily gives up his individual expression, stales his artistic abilities, and diminishes his creative thinking. He slowly gives up his thoughts, beliefs and desires, and swaps them for those of warp-minded TV producers. In exchange, he receives countless suggestions and advice most contrary to human nature, indirect and subliminal messages that are at best immoral. These endless money-hungry opportunists viciously play tug-of-war with the mind and body, all the while stoking emotions and preying on insecurities.

Television and especially advertisement producers have been extremely successful in devising clever ways to compel one to adopt to their ever-changing standards, simply by suggesting that if you don't have their product there's something wrong with you, you're not good enough, you are incomplete, and, if you want to be the best you must have *'this'*!

Duped into a stupor by hours of this *'programming'*, the excessive TV viewer is unable to think intelligently by himself or for himself. The man with the small-penis complex is especially susceptible, swallowing hours upon hours of stereotypes and notions of perfection, constantly comparing himself, just to fall short in another area, and yet another.

One era of television was highly influential in the success of convincing Americans that they weren't good enough – the hit TV show *Baywatch*. At the time it was the most-watched number one re-run around the world. But why do you think that was?

Of course, you could argue that the beautiful, buxom, irreplaceable co-star, Pamela Anderson is mostly responsible for its universal popularity and success. Some will swear it's the sexy hunks – David Hasselhoff and his male co-stars - that compelled the loyal fans to keep tuning in. While others support a more general opinion, emphasizing the background scenes of sexy scantily-clad bathing beauties and beaus strutting and frolicking around the beach as background extras.

According to the American standards of beauty and perfection, all the cast members of *Baywatch* fall short of... absolutely nothing! Gorgeous desirable women: big-breasted blondes and beautiful brunettes with full lips, pretty eyes, svelte waistlines, and cute little tight derrieres.

Sounds good. But the problem is, the producers only ever show these women being courted by their equally beautiful male counterparts: hunky men with chiseled faces, ripped abdominals and broad chests and shoulders sculpted to a 10.

In essence, these men and women are looked upon as flawless, perfect and to-die-for. Since the man with a small-penis complex usually carries a seriously poor self-image to begin with, the not-so-subtle message these perfect specimens convey is custom-made to make him feel inadequate, insufficient, and unequal to what is required. His insecurities grow deeper as he interprets from watching the show that he must be a gorgeous hunk in order to have a *Baywatch*-beauty type of girl.

Therefore, I strongly encourage you to avoid watching *Baywatch* re-runs and other shows like it that seem designed to make you feel worse about yourself. The last things you need are undermining influences like this. So keep an eye on your TV-dependency. It only breeds stress and misery, which could lead you into a downward spiral of self-hate, before you have a chance to change the channel.

46. Don't Blame It On Your Race Or Ethnicity.

Ethnic image and social pressures influence our body image. But even more so influencing a man's psychobiology are his racial myths and images. Though sometimes, said myths about specific racial groups are in part true, many times they are just that, myths! A bunch of false rumors, and wishful thinking.

When it comes to penis size these racial/ethnic images and pressures are magnified. Mainly because society-at-large carries around preconceived notions that certain ethnic groups have bigger penises than others. One popular notion (and myth) is that African men have the largest penises, Asian men have the smallest penises, and European and Hispanic men fall somewhere in the middle. This is not true!

These myths and stereotypes may hold for certain men, but just think of how African men feel who don't have large penises, and in fact have quite small penises, and therefore can't live up to their African myth.

Or even worse, imagine Asian men having any size penis, yet going through society constantly aware that society-at-large looks upon them as having small penises!

Just imagine the mental devastation both these men could suffer, worrying about other people's expectations based on their race. Not to mention, the loss of self-esteem and social esteem. The effects of having to go through life feeling you have a little penis could weigh heavily on a man's sense of masculinity, no matter what racial, ethnical, or cultural background one has. And whether or not that particular background has a penis myth attached to it.

47. Blame Men For The Bad Reputation Of Your Small Penis, Not Women!

Surprisingly, it is not women who are giving little penises a bad name. It was never women who said, *"The bigger a man's penis is, the better a lover he is."*

It was never women who started saying, *"The larger a man's dick is the more manly he is."*

And it is not women who are causing men to believe their little penises are incapable of bringing them to climax. It's men.

Men are the real culprits. Men are the initiators of all the little-penis jokes, stereotypes, myths and cants. The belittling of one man by another comes from man's huge but fragile ego and competitive nature. Not to mention his own insecurities about a woman's perception of himself.

Men with big penises intentionally tease men with smaller penises in an attempt to elevate themselves above the men they tease, or just to try to feel better about themselves, if only for the moment. In many cases, a man with a larger penis will launch an offensive tease attack on a man he knows or believes has a small penis (probably because he doesn't see it bulging out of the crotch of his pants); especially if the man with the small penis intimidates him with intelligence and knowledge, or worse yet, challenges his masculinity or questions his manhood; or if he sees the man with the smaller penis with somewhat of a *playboy* status – rounding up a bunch of women for no apparent *physical* reason.

This *'penis-teasing'* began and only used to go on in the circles of men, where there was more laughing than anything, and less emotional harm done. Back then, the playing field was level, the sexual revolution was not yet televised or mass publicized and penis-teasing was looked at as just another weird form of male bonding.

But, to lengthen the *'short end of the stick'*, every man seemed to possess something that allowed him to compensate for where he lacked – be that compensation a good sense of humor, secure financial status, a great personality, a nice body, advanced education or intelligence, or a big dick... And we little penis-insecure men prayed, *'Heaven help us'* if a man got blessed with a big dick and other qualities on top of it!

But only when men imagined a more fierce competition for the opposite sex, and sensitive feelings and emotions became more involved, did men begin to un-equal the playing field by allowing women to actively listen and take part in these once-exclusive discussions men indulged themselves in.

Men wanted women to sort of quietly listen to their conversations, heated discussions, and unfamiliar talk, while at the same time observe each man's individual mannerisms, gestures and behaviors. In this way, men intended to charm and flatter the women through his assertiveness in taking charge of the group; his education in bringing logic and wisdom to the discussion, his confidence in dealing with other men and handling situations, real and imagined. But most of all, he intended to captivate the woman by exuding 100% masculinity, total sensitivity and subtle sex appeal.

But if a man thought the women showed no interest in him, and he believed he had no real surface qualities, yet placed his edge in his large penis, he would change the conversation towards sexuality, in an attempt to appeal to the women's base nature. As long as the woman didn't verbally object to the change, he could care less how other men felt. If another man showed signs of frustration over the topic, the first man would verbally attribute this discomfort to a lack of confidence in his sexual ability. It's just like in the animal kingdom; a dominant male shows aggression toward the other males just so he can have a chance to mate with the female.

As the years have gone by, this has become the norm. Conversation in men's social circles has become much looser in the presence of women. Everyone is vying for the attention of the ladies, which influences what the guys say. Conversations of raunchy, explicit sexuality often become the main topic.

Even attire by both sexes has become more revealing and figure-flattering. Since larger penises imprint clothes more prominently, women have become more sexually focused on them. They get even more excited when a man touches or scratches his crotch, or dwells on what he could and would do with his large penis.

Consequently, little penises got less respect, and talk of 'em got even less attention. To make matters worse, it's men who are constantly creating and producing movies, books, magazines, TV sitcoms and talk shows that promote big anatomy as a prerequisite for a man. It naturally follows that small anatomy is ridiculed, laughed at, and made the butt of jokes. Nowadays, when it comes to making fun of a man for having a little penis, women are at the forefront – but guess who encouraged them to do so?

48. Relinquish Bad Memories Of The Past.

It seems that an irresistible force compels our minds to rehash old memories. Some are pleasant; but most, especially in our case, are unpleasant. We hate them because they promote inhibiting fear about our future relationships with women.

Though mostly undetected by women, we experience feelings of anxiety and agitation brought on by past memories of sexual episodes that were not in harmony with our desired performance. We persist getting stuck in these memories... but why?

Nothing can be gotten from them but mental harm. It can't be stressed enough that those past memories are stale. Yesterday's memories are fast spoiling and we cannot live on spoiled matter. We must release the past and become anew. In order to move forward in our relationships with women, we must first rid our minds of those lingering injuries. Then, and only then, can the healing process begin.

49. Don't Stress Over It Much. Anxiety Disorder Could Develop.

Everybody knows what its like to feel anxious. Whether it is the butterflies in your stomach before a first date or initial sex with someone, the tension you feel when your boss is angry, or the way your heart pounds if you're in danger, anxiety rouses you to action, it gears you up to face a threatening situation. In general it helps you cope.

But if you have an anxiety disorder, this potentially helpful emotion can do just the opposite – it can keep you from coping and disrupt your daily life. An anxiety disorder isn't just a case of 'nerves'. It is an illness, often related to the biological and anatomical makeup and life experiences of the individual, and it frequently runs in families.

There are several types of anxiety disorders, even sexual. Men with little-penis anxiety may feel anxious most of the time, without any apparent reason, and consequently avoid intimacy and sexual encounters.

Or the anxious feelings may be so uncomfortable that to counter them one may resort to self-medication through drugs, alcohol or food. You may even have occasional bouts of anxiety so intense they terrify and immobilize you.

Anxiety disorders are the most common of all mental disorders. Many believe incorrectly that individuals should be able to overcome the symptoms by sheer willpower. Wishing away the symptoms of an anxiety disorder does not work, but there are treatments that can help.

For more information contact:

National Institute of Mental Health, Info Services, Depression: 1-800-421-4211

Panic and other Anxiety Disorders: 1-800-647-2642
http://www.nimh.nih.gov

50. Consult Other Guys With The Same Damn Problem.

You know the old saying, "misery loves company" – need I say more? I mean, that there just 'bout wraps it up. Because no one wants to feel like they're the only one in the world (or, better yet, the only one they know) suffering from a particular mental or physical problem.

Especially in this case, men love to know that other men are going through the exact same thing. They absolutely love it! And even though it's cruel to find relief and humor in someone else's *'confidence-crusher'*, men actually delight in the news, especially if the guy's good-looking. Oh yeah, that's the *best*, ain't it? Although he may not be competing with his newfound anatomical twin, it seems to level the playing field and restore some lost confidence.

For penis-insecure men, the desire to be the same size as 'most' men is mainly a mental game. In an odd way, by fulfilling that desire (that is, knowing of other men with the same size) they swear it would allow them to maintain a safe level of macho image.

That's why it is extremely important for penis-insecure men to purposely seek out other men who feel the same way. And preferably attend regular meetings and group therapy with the fellahs with penis insecurity as the main subject – and it wouldn't hurt to have a few women in the group, too.

Women would be helpful to include in these discussions because the men could get a feminine perspective to bounce back off. The women could talk about their own personal experience or offer a general female outlook on the subject, declaring whether his insecurity is necessary or warranted. Because unlike men, who tend to think with their little head instead of their brains, women are better able to see things in perspective relevant to this subject.

Women are able to instinctively draw back on past or current relationship experiences and quickly determine whether the man's penis size had any bearing on holding the relationship together. Most often the answer would be a clear 'no'.

Without talking to others on the issue, tension, frustration and severe stress can mount and result in self-inflicted injury, both mental and physical. So group therapy, or just talking to another man with the same concerns, will definitely have a positive effect. When men talk about it, they often find themselves laughing and joking about the very thing that stressed them so. Even if after talking with others the insecurity still persists (and it probably will), chances are it will no longer totally influence his self-esteem because he'll have gained some much-needed perspective.

51. Attend A Self-Help Group.

One proven source of relief from stress, depression and low self-esteem that is almost always overlooked is attending a self-help group. Self-help groups have been known to do wonders for individuals who suffer all kinds of personal problems, from emotional instability to negative addictive behavior to various insecurities.

Although some men with small-penis complexes are not very sociable people, they are quite friendly people and will be friends with just about anybody who likes them. This friendly nature makes it easy for them to be around people of the group who may be from different backgrounds and have different personalities. It is not so important to find a group that has the exact same problems you have. But it is important to link up with a group of people who share like-minded support in the way of listening attentively to an individual's problems or hang-ups, and coming together in a group effort to try and find practical solutions, or at least a common understanding.

It is important to network with members of your group and other groups who share your experiences and emotions, although maybe not from the same causes or reasons. Keeping in constant contact with the group through in-person meetings or in touch via telephone is an excellent way to express and relieve built-up tensions and pent-up frustrations. It's also a good way to approach self-help and self-healing via alternative medicine, and without any medicine.

Attending and participating in regular meetings lets the other members know you are genuinely concerned about their well-being too. In many ways, group therapy members work together as a team on the popular notions that *"two heads are better than one"* and *"team membership can influence individual concept"*. This old strategy is very effective and beneficial for the individual absorbed by his issues. Because often times the troubled individual gets trapped in his /her own illogic, and resorts to actions that could be harmful.

In the group you need to have open dialogue, specifically about what the expectations are for the members, and the issue you are seeking help with. Important to your success with the group will come from your compatibility with the group as a whole, because this can affect your commitment to attending regularly. Remember to take part in reflective thinking and active listening. The advice and information you get, along with human concern and emotional support you receive, are truly invaluable. Self-help groups are excellent for your spirit!

52. Talk To A Sex Therapist.

If you often feel stressed out or find yourself in deep depression and are extremely troubled by the belief the fact or idea that your penis is too small, then a helpful thing might be to seek professional counseling from a sex therapist. A sex therapist is a specialist whose field of expertise lies in sexuality and human sexual behavior. They administer therapy in an attempt to cure, remedy, or treat mental disease, emotional and physical disorders attributed to one's sexuality, such as sexual anxiety and premature ejaculation, negative and harmful sexual compulsions, sexual phobias and sexual depression.

Counseling from a sex therapist has been very helpful to many men with small penises who suffered sexual trauma at one time or another in their lives – especially a painful emotional sexual experience that had a lasting psychological effect. It can be easier to talk out and express personal and emotional problems with a doctor or therapist rather than family and friend. A major reason is that it's very impersonal, and the therapist is objective. Although, part of the job of a sex therapist is to probe deeply into the consciousness and emotional psyche of a person to get to the root of the problem by digging out the innermost thoughts and intimate feelings, the therapist-patient relationship is virtually nonexistent outside the office.

Unlike family and close friends, the sex therapist is not invested in developing a closer relationship and becoming part of your daily life. The relationship is strictly professional and allows you to retain your dignity and integrity – still feeling complete with self-esteem intact, and not leaving you feeling unnecessarily exposed and vulnerable.

If you decide to try it, choose carefully and wisely –
preferably, a therapist of repute and not under the age of forty.
Whether male or female, is at your discretion. But just to get a
more rounded view and a different perspective, try both.

In any event, try to look beyond the surface of their
occupational title and sincerely try to understand what is being
said. And remember to speak up, be frank and up-front. Let the
therapist know exactly how your past sexual experiences and
present state of mind are affecting you. Take your time, and be
truthful. Be sure the time spent with your therapist is used
wisely – it can get expensive! But the information and
professional advice you receive could be invaluable. It could
help rid you of your recurring addictive emotional troubles that
could linger as long as your heart and mind are not clear.

If you know your small penis is causing you emotional chaos
as well as trouble with your sex life, but persist in
procrastinating in making an appointment with a sex therapist,
then know that the very start of your healing process begins
with your own actions. Take a serious look at how often you
create excuses not to do the things you know could make your
life better.

53. Use Aphrodisiacs.

An aphrodisiac could be any drug or agent arousing and or
increasing sexual desire. An aphrodisiac probably wont make
your penis bigger, but it can assist you in maintaining a long-
lasting erection that will undoubtedly enable you to give your
women extended pleasure during lovemaking. And when it
comes to lovemaking, extended pleasure is treasure! – and
rated much higher than an extended penis.

The use of aphrodisiacs around the world is ever-increasing.
And the marketing, production, and new claims of products
having an aphrodisiac effect are even more so. Funny thing is
though, no one thing and nobody has a monopoly on what an
aphrodisiac is... for it can be anything... a drug, a particular

food or drink, a song, a certain place, or even another person!

An aphrodisiac is anything that is able to produce a result that is sexually stimulating – whether that be in the form of an erection or the desire to have sex. A few of the more popular products that are said, or have been proven, to have an aphrodisiac effect are:

Ginseng – a Chinese root herb, similar in appearance to ginger.

Wellbutrin – an antidepressant in many cases found to improve sexual performance and increase sexual desire by stimulating the libido.

Yohimbe – a chemical derived from the bark of the West African tree, *corynanthe yohimbe*.

Ginseng is a root available in tea products, pills and capsule forms. Ginseng has positive effects on fighting depression and stress; it reduces drowsiness and fatigue, and makes you feel more spirited and alive. Taking ginseng can also reduce the stress effects of rigorous and strenuous exercise.

The drug Wellbutrin is an antidepressant and in many cases has been found to improve one's sexual performance and increase sexual desire by stimulating the libido.

Yohimbine has an extended history as an aphrodisiac. It's prescribed for impotence caused by diabetes and vascular disease. And it also works well for men who suffer form 'psychogenic impotence' – psychological troubles and mental conflicts – usually sexual hang-ups and poor past performances (real or imagined) that linger in the mind and keep men from getting erections.

Clinical studies show that yohimbine has a success rate of restoring erections in up to a third of impotent men. The success rate more than doubles that in men who had impotence to a lesser degree. It also works well for men who don't complain of any sexually debilitating problems. Mild side effects of headache, dizziness, anxiety and nausea have been reported. Fortunately they go away within two days of discontinued use of the drug.

Yohimbine is sold over-the-counter in health food stores and pharmacies. It's manufactured as tea products, capsules and pills, and sold under the names *Yocon*, *Yohimex*, and *Aprodyne*. But to know the correct dosage, a doctor should be consulted.

You could also try more or larger servings of certain foods that friends have said caused an aphrodisiac effect on them. Here's a few I've heard of and have tried myself to induce immediate erections:

- 4 or 5 tablespoons of honey, straight.
- 4 or 5 tablespoons of creamy peanut butter.
- 2 or 3 plain Hershey chocolate bars.

There are some drugs which are self-injected directly into the penis that will produce an erection – but painful or not, just the thought of that procedure makes my penis withdraw in cowardice, while holding up two balls to block the dickhead entrance.

Still, many guys are just fed-up with the so-called *mythical* or *natural* aphrodisiacs said to produce an erection: certain vitamins, various roots and herbal teas. They're expensive, they take too long to work, you have to consume too much, and they're too hard to find. Then, some only work the first couple of times you ingest it, (if they work at all). And certain mixtures of Yohimbine have even worked against getting an erection.

We just want a miracle drug! That magic pill, with minimal non-threatening side effects. Well, that ain't here yet... but, chemists have managed to conjure-up some "pixy dust", until...

They call them Viagra, Cialis, Levitra and ExtenZe. These new products are virtually stealing the show because they are more reliable to give you that *guaranteed* erection you need – RIGHT NOW! I must say; I tried them, I like them, I take them.

All four are erectile dysfunction drugs that increase blood flow to the penis.

All give you harder and more frequent erections.

All can help improve your sexual life by enhancing desire,

pleasure and performance.

Viagra lasts about 4 hours and delays orgasm. Side effects can include headache, dizziness and blindness.

Levitra lasts about 4 hours and has fewer and less severe side effects.

Cialis lasts about 36 hours but does not impede orgasm. Side effects can include headache, muscle ache, and blurred vision.

ExtenZe claims that it is 100% safe, guaranteed, and will increase the size of your penis.

Piggin'-out on some sweets seems to be the safest way to a quick erection. But we ain't tryin' to get fat on someone else's penis diet!

54. Read Magazines And Other Periodicals Catering To Women.

If a woman could have one wished-for quality in a man, but in return for that wish, must forgive the slight mental, emotional, or physical flaw the man believes he has, that one wish would be: *"I wish he would hear me, listen to me, pay attention to me, and understand me!"* The absence of this rare quality will continue to go down in history as a *major complaint women have about men* for as long as humans walk this earth.

Throughout their lives, most men barely contemplate the fact that women are practically a different species – complicated in emotions, feelings, and diverse patterns of thought. This is why so many men don't relate well to women, other than physical, sexual penetration. It naturally follows that when women talk to men, men don't hear them. They don't listen to their complaints, and they don't understand their problems. Funny thing is, for the most part, women tell us all of their problems. Catch is, they're very subtle and indirect, and this information is usually accompanied with nagging, arguing, and sudden mood swings. This roundabout type of communication women use for many reasons, some of which are:

1. When she tells you straight-out what the problem is, you don't respond favorably, if you respond at all.

2. She's still expecting what you promised a long time ago, while resenting that you haven't delivered.

3. You're supposed to be a mind reader...

4. She expects that you already know *something* about a woman.

5. You're a jerk!

Since we ordinary men fall short in yet another area of understanding women, about the best thing we could do to educate ourselves and flatter her at the same time, is to learn more about women and how they operate.

One practical method is to read magazines such as *Essence, Shape, Cosmo, Psychology Today,* and other periodicals catering to women. Although compact, these monthly magazines immensely inform their readers on the issues of women from A to Z. From reading, one will come to know that women so desperately want their man to know their likes, dislikes, turn-ons, turn-offs, and why their moods swing. And to understand and be sensitive when she seems to voluntarily get on the emotional roller coaster at least once a week!

The ads also cover in-depth information on a woman's total sexuality. And even go so far as publishing full pages of *"Questions and Answers"* from actual subscribers about their personal problems.

One personal problem women often complain about, is the lack of sexual compatibility in their relationships. Sexual compatibility is crucial to a woman. Men need to understand that sexual compatibility is not just if he thinks his penis fits her vagina perfectly. Or, if he succeeds in bringing her to climax before he does. The key to sexual compatibility is *sexual respect.* And sexual respect implies trying to ascertain what's liked. What's desired. What's annoying. And what's very much appreciated.

Many couples make the huge mistake of expecting each other

to intuitively know what the other wants, when neither is a mind reader. It cannot be stressed enough: *"If there's something you want, say so!"* It's best to talk about it sooner than later – it could save the spice in your sexual relationship – or your sex life all together.

And another thing that might inspire you to read up: women are turned on by men who understand the female anatomy. Why do you think so many doctors and male gynecologists get the pick of their desire? But even though you may not be a professional, women still want men to know, and they appreciate a man who makes an effort to learn what pleases his woman sexually, and what does not. It also shows a man is comfortable with a woman's sexuality, and not intimidated by it! And shows he's willing to explore all of her, and not just rush to intercourse.

Informative women's magazines and related publications also address the much debated, yet mysterious *G-spot*, and explain how important the clitoris is to a woman's orgasm.

But one equally important issue is women's illnesses and diseases. Should your woman ever be subjected to any, just think of the sound advice you could give her on treatments, and other day-to day care; not to mention the invaluable emotional support that's so vital to her healing process! Truly bond-strengthening.

55. If A Woman Tells You That Your Size is Fine, Believe Her!

Probably the worse part of the 'disease' of small-penis complex, is that it is mostly a mental disorder that can greatly inhibit the mind from pleasurable and positive thoughts about sex and one's performance. This can also lead to a warped sense and unhealthy concept about sex and one's sexuality.

Case in point: when the man with the small-penis complex is having sexual relations with a woman, this mental disorder compels him to know whether or not she thinks his penis size is alright. The disease of the disorder comes in on the fact that even when the woman says his size is fine, he doesn't believe her!

A small percentage of his disbelief isn't without reason... for he knows that women are aware that a huge part of a man's sexual esteem lies in his penis size; and just to protect that fragile male ego, she will often lie or suppress her true feelings.

Problem is, the women are not always lying, but he tends not to trust any of them, no matter how much she appears to be enjoying sex with him. Solely behind his small-penis complex, he almost takes on the emotions and insecurities of a woman, constantly needing reassurance from the woman's words or actions that his penis is okay. But the need for verbal reassurance could end up doing more harm than good.

The relationship might be largely based on honesty, and the woman could be too honest for her own good. If so, when he asks that question, and she sincerely thinks his penis is small, she will say so.... and his fragile ego and sense of well-being in the relationship will quickly fall apart.

Still, assuming the woman really does think his penis is too small (yet she's honest, but compassionate), the best answer he could hope for is, *"Your penis size is okay."* Or, *"The size of your penis is fine."* Even this type of answer can do more harm than good. Because if a woman uses the terms *"okay"* or *"fine"* to rate his penis size, his insecurities will translate that into an average of C+ at best, which leaves room for improvement. But technically, the word *'fine'* can also mean *'very good'* or *'better than average'*. He'll take it according to how she says it, but his complex might twist it into the most negative possible interpretation.

So, just to be safe, don't ask. But if you feel compelled to, then believe her when she tells you your penis size is *fine*, 'cause more than likely, it is. Even if she does think you're too small, as long as she isn't afraid of you and you continue to treat her with tender loving care, kindness, and respect, she's gonna stick it out with you until you prove yourself otherwise.

But be careful of needing too much reassurance and mistreating her on top of that even if the mistreatment be only criticism of her outward appearance like her weight or her breast size. Because for most women, criticism of their appearance is the most hurtful and emotional criticism they will ever endure. So, if you are mistreating her in this way, be on guard, 'cause she could be eager for payback! She's gonna want to hurt you as bad as she can without putting her hands on you, and without causing any real physical pain. And of course, the best and most effective way to hurt a man without real physical harm is to tell him his dick is too small!

So if you're a man who needs reassurance on your penis size, be sure you give her reassurance on her insecurities. But don't get too comfortable about discussing your insecurities with your mate … you could sabotage the relationship. Because a woman is looking for a man who can comfort her more than she has to comfort him.

PART VIII:

SMALL MEASUREMENTS CAN LEAD TO DRASTIC MEASURES

56. Don't Believe A Blow-Up Device Can Make It Bigger.

If you're like most men, at one time or another you've browsed the pages of sexually explicit magazines, such as *Penthouse* and *Hustler*, and come across those advertisements for penis blow-up devices. These ads are usually printed near the back in the last few pages of the magazine, along with sexually explicit personal ads and 900 numbers.

These ads are very attractive, and act as an emotional magnet for men who suffer from small-penis complex. Reason being, these ads state with enthusiasm that a man could add at least 3 inches to his penis almost immediately, just by using this device, and without invasive surgery. The ads also stress that their penis blow-up devices are very safe and hazard-free, and the best thing about it is that you can use this do-it-yourself device to get a bigger and fuller penis right in the comfort of your own home!

Man! What penis-insecure gentleman wouldn't be moved by these types of advertisements? For he sees this as a potential quick fix for his mental, emotional and physical inadequacy. The men who buy these products, or seriously consider buying them, are men who have become fed up with having a little penis and are ready to do something about it. They have become so vulnerable; they'll try almost anything with minimal side effects, or just short of major surgery.

Remember *Sea Monkeys* and the *X-Ray Glasses*? Problem is, these gimmicks don't work like the advertisements portray they will. The devices do not and cannot add inches or increase the size of a man's penis beyond his natural full erection. So all in all, the penis blow-up device is just another gimmick created by the many money-hungry opportunists who seek new ways to prey on the sensitive emotions of insecure people.

However, although you'll get gypped outta your intended purpose, it may not be a total loss, because if you often find it difficult to obtain an erection, the penis blow-up device can be a pretty trustworthy assistant. Technically, the penis blow-up device is a vacuum device that induces vacuum constriction, or negative pressure, around the penis. The ingenuity in which the way they work is quite simple: You fit a clear plastic cylinder-shaped object over your limp penis, make sure you have a tight air seal, and then with the hand pump (or electric pump) start pumping all the air out of the cylinder. This negative pressure, or "pump down" action, causes the penis to become engorged with blood, thereby producing an erection. Once your erection is full as it seems it's gonna get (because it won't get as firm as your natural erection), then you slip a rubber band-like constriction ring off the end of the cylinder and over the base of your erection (butting up against your pelvis) and trapping the blood in your penis.

The very next thing you do is… well… I think you know how to handle it from here! But while you're handling your manly duty, one very important rule must be observed: keep track of the time (the actual minutes the constriction ring is around your penis) because this constriction ring acts like a tourniquet, and you don't want to leave a tourniquet on your most invaluable tool indefinitely, 'cause you could risk losing it! So never leave it on more than 30 minutes, no matter how good it gets. And only leave it on about half that time if you already have vascular problems. The erection you get is not a full rock-hard erection either, but hard enough to get inside the vagina, which is usually all the head start most men need to firm up.

But like everything that seems to do some good for us almost always has its downfalls, the most common complaints are that it's a little painful or uncomfortable because of the constriction of blood and skin. And minor bruises from the device (with continued use) causes spot marks on the penis – but will go a way as use is discontinued. One more thing... because the urethra is squeezed during the process, ejaculation becomes difficult.

57. Consider Surgery: Fat Transfer To Your Penis.

Most men that suffer from small-penis complex have tried numerous physical exercises and other related penis-enlargement techniques to the point of disappointment and frustration, simply because they just don't work. These guys have tried it all and they're tired of it all. No wonder more and more men are getting information and advice about penis-enlargement surgery.

There are different procedures that can be performed. But to keep it simple let's put the focus on just two. Because it is relatively safe and a simple procedure we will tell you about penis- enlargement involving your own anatomy, and another procedure involving you own fat cells. There are two separate procedures, lengthening and girth enhancement, that can be done without the use of implants or other foreign materials.

In the lengthening procedure, the suspensory ligament which connects the penis to the pubic bone is released, allowing access to the section of the penis hidden behind the skin wall. The surgeon is now able to extend the length of the penis in proportion to the length the organ's internal section. Now that the additional erectile tissue is exposed, the ligament must be reattached to prevent retraction. Then, to cover the newly-exposed section, a flap of skin from in front of the pubic bone is brought down. Actual length gain depends on the individual patient's anatomy and cannot be predicted. The individual's suspensory ligament is the limiting factor. But it generally increases from 1 to 2-1/2 inches.

In the girth enhancement procedure, fat cells from the patient's lower abdomen are transferred into the tissue region between the skin and the erectile tissue of the penis. Using the patient's own fat cells is preferred, because they don't run the risk of getting rejected by the body. Circumference increase is generally thirty to fifty percent.

In each procedure, increases will be in both the flaccid and erect state (Okay, guys, stop getting excited! You haven't had the surgery yet), but length gain in the flaccid state is usually greater. Each procedure takes about half an hour.

58. Consider Surgery: Penile Implant.

Ouch! Come on; is it really all that bad? No, seriously though? 'Cause this is major, major surgery we're talking about!

Just so you know, penile implant surgery is mainly intended for the treatment of impotence – men who are unable to engage in sexual intercourse, or often have difficulty engaging in sexual intercourse because of an inability to have an erection. This is not minor surgery. And it is not 'casual' surgery, like getting a nose job people get because of teasing throughout adolescence. Although penile implant surgery has been performed for many different reasons, its targeted candidates are usually men who have become impotent because of injury, pelvic surgery for prostate cancer, illnesses such as heart disease, Peyronie's disease (bent penis), spinal cord injuries, and chronic alcoholism.

But recently, a growing number of men have been getting the surgery performed, and many others have seriously contemplated it. Many for reasons not listed above – even for reasons quite vain and outright ridiculous.

Plastic surgeons have reported cases where men have gotten the surgery, or wanted to have it done, only because one or two women told them their penis is too small. And some cases where men have heard a publicized statement regarding the average penis size, and to their dismay found that theirs was a couple of inches shorter, became desperate to have the surgery done.

For face value, these two reasons are immature and not well thought-out. Mainly because once the surgery is done, it's done... ain't no turning back! You can't just reverse the process (for whatever reason) and revert back to normal life as it was. Because this type of surgery often alters normal blood flow to the penis, therefore, without the implant you may never be able to get an erection on your own ever again. So as you see, it's a serious decision to contemplate. That said, penile implants do have a high success rate.

There are over a dozen types on the market, but all are in either of two categories: 'inflatable' and 'non-inflatable'. Inflatable implants are more life-like, because they can be inflated and deflated. This is done by means of a tiny pump, a storage reservoir, and a pair of rod-like inflatable cylinders that are implanted in the shaft of the penis. When you want an erection you simply press the pump with your finger; that releases fluid from the reservoir into the implants (cylinder rods) producing an erection. And when you've had enough of your erection, you press that deflating valve, the fluid returns back to the reservoir, and the penis gets limp again.

The latest designs of penis inflatable implants allow surgical procedures to be simpler because the pump and the reservoir are both built into the implant itself. Like most new technology, the devices are getting smaller and more compact (which is ironic, since our wish is to have a *bigger* penis - not smaller). And these new devices were not exempt – making them hold less fluid, and the erection is less firm than previous models.

Non-inflatable implants are the simplest and least expensive. A pair of bendable rods is implanted side by side into the two long narrow erectile chambers that lie inside the penis. The material used for the rods are sometimes silicon rubber with a bendable or hinged metallic core. When you're ready for sex, just bend them outward, and when you're done, bend them back. The worst thing about this implant is that it remains permanently stiff. It still can be concealed under clothes, though. But in public restrooms and locker rooms it can be obvious.

Non-inflatable can sometimes be implanted with a local

anesthetic. In some centers, patients are hospitalized for two or three days to give them intensive antibiotic therapy before, during and after the operation. And sexual intercourse is usually prohibited for a month after surgery. The rate of malfunction is less than five percent, and infection rates are about 2 to 3 percent according to recent studies.

59. If You're Thinking About Surgery, Ask A Few Questions Beforehand.

If you're unsure about what specific questions to ask, then request a list of the most frequently asked questions. And also questions that should be of concern but are not usually asked. Here are some other general questions you might want to get answered before going any further:

1. What are the chances of complications?
2. What kind of complications?
3. Is there a risk of loss of sensitivity? Or worse, impotence?
4. Is there any discomfort after my body is completely healed?
5. After surgery, approximately how long before I can start having sex?
6. When can I return to work?
7. Will there be a noticeable scar or any other sign I had the procedure done?
8. What are my chances for improvement?
9. Are my particular desired results obtainable?
10. What are the different types of procedures done?
11. Can more than one procedure be done at once?
12. Do men usually choose more than one procedure?
13. Can you repeat a procedure I had already gotten from another doctor, but didn't like the results?
14. Will surgery make me a better lover?
And last but not least; *how much does it cost?*

60. If You're Planning On Surgery, Don't Forget To Bring Your Wallet.

Desiring a bigger penis and talking about the different procedures that can be performed is one thing. But actually having the money it costs for certain procedures could be outta the ballpark. That's right baby, it costs to be the boss!

If you were thinking about a procedure that will leave you average to well-endowed, get ready for a nice well-endowed fee. If you're hoping to be more like Long John Silver, prepare yourself for a silver platinum price.

Not going too deep, let's talk about the money it costs for enhancement procedures via fat transfer. Length and girth enhancement by liposuction fat transfer costs around $6,000. Another procedure, payable in advance, is length and girth enhancement through dermal fat transfer. It also costs around $6,000.

You may wanna just do lengthening alone – the price for that it is $3,900. Or you may think you just need a little help in the girth department, only. Its price is the same, $3,900. If after allowable healing time has passed, and you still want your penis to be bigger, the cost is another $3,900. Oh yeah, Buddy! It's like owning a boat... b.o.a.t. That is, *break-out-another-thousand*. And expect to pay a reservation fee of five hundred dollars, payable at the time the surgery is scheduled. This fee is fully refundable up to one week before surgery, but not after that. Most insurance policies will not cover these enhancement surgeries. However, if you have a condition called congenital micro penis (erect length 3-1/2 inches or less) you could be in luck. Good luck!

61. Get Married... Quick!

Having a small penis in itself could be the most prominent source of negative body image. If these feelings are strong enough, it's only reasonable to conclude that they may affect some men's decisions about having sexual encounters and intimacies with women. In spite of this pitiful attitude some men will no doubt take, these men would like no more than to have healthy, loving, intimate sexual relationships as do many other men who don't have a small-penis complex. In seeking relief for their deeply-rooted emotional feelings about their insecurities, these men often think up or consider extreme ideas that are medically known to be potentially dangerous and definitely unhealthy.

But the one simple solution that seems to dangle right in front of their faces, though many won't take heed of is *marriage*! Men who suffer from this penis inferiority complex need to stop wasting precious years of their lives running from this girl to that girl only to hear that this girl doesn't want a second date and that girl doesn't want to commit! The winning solution is to get married... but quick.

We all know many women want to be married above all else. Seek someone you can trust, whom you can confide in, and whom you can communicate your insecurities to. A woman who will be mindful and sensitive to your emotional needs. A woman who is meek and humble. And a woman who will pledge her faithful devotion to you and only you.

Getting married is one of the most respected responsibilities we men could undertake. And there are many benefits and advantages. For instance, let's take the sex factor: hot, steamy, passionate, yet safe and compatible sex between two who love and adore one another. Sex at your beck and call, virtually anytime you desire. Sex with someone who anxiously anticipates you and your penis. And sex with someone who loves you and your size.

Seems like a 'no-brainer', huh?

62. Marry A Woman In Prison.

For a man with a small-penis complex this could be just the ego-booster he needs. After a couple of years behind bars, most of these women find their standards of an ideal man substantially dropping. Facial appearance and physical make-up are characteristics rarely sought, and they both play a backseat role to everything else a relationship could offer. One advantage is, you can virtually choose from the cream of the crop. And the good thing is, that 'ol cliché, about how the prettier a girl is, the crazier she is. I mean, that's gotta translate into a more serious crime for a longer *time*. Which may be better for you because now you've got a little more time to figure out what you really want to do with this girl; stay with her or marry her cell-mate.

And of course, there are plenty of average-looking women in prison, not all of who are uncaring, callous and involved in a life of crime.

Many men with penis insecurity often involve themselves in spurious or temporal relationships for fear of female abandonment. Therefore, they might want to seek more stable relationships where they have more control over the situation. Marriage with a woman in prison offers both. In this kind of relationship, the man feels very stable and secure because he knows where she is every minute of the day and what she's *not* doing. Secure, because he knows there are no other men in her life and she makes him feel she absolutely adores everything about him. Even if there was a faint chance of another man in her life, he at least knows she is not sleeping with him. He also feels a sense of control because he can basically dictate the tone and pace of their relationship; it's up to him for the two of them to get together physically, emotionally and sexually.

But along with this seemingly good trade-off comes a few disadvantages: there are set times for phone calls – you can't reach out to your prison bride around the clock. Visiting hours are also regulated. Non-conjugal visits are usually between 8A.M. and 3:30P.M. Conjugal visits, unsupervised by prison officials, in which sexual intercourse can take place, last two days running. But they can vary in schedule from once every few weeks to once in three months.

Another major disadvantage is a daily one: The woman won't

be there to cook meals for her husband, nor will she be there for him to reach out to in his time of emotional need or physical desire. And the husband will be expected to maintain a life of celibacy until he and his wife come together for conjugal visits. So, as you can see, this type of relationship demands a huge amount of strength and discipline. And could only come from an extraordinary man with a tremendous sense of commitment.

63. Settle For No Less Than A Virgin.

This is one suggestion I think most penis-size insecure men would love to take on. The biggest problem with this advice is almost always the same; where to find one? ...especially nowadays. We are living in a sex-preoccupied era. It would seem a most difficult task to actually find a virgin – one of 'age' that is. Or even a woman who's tried other acts of sexual gratification without actually having experienced vaginal intercourse. But trust me, they're out there. You just have to know where to look.

Just ask yourself: *"If I were a virgin, where would I hangout?"* And you'd probably come to some reasonable answers, like the church, the library, the beaches, and social family gatherings.

Churches – because, well, virgins are always expected to be in church, right? And it's probably where a virgin can feel most at home. In part, because church people tend to reverence virgins for their purity and innocence.

Libraries – because virgins are thought to be somewhat nerdy, and more into school and studying.

Beaches – beaches? Yeah, beaches. Because human innocence always flirts with temptation. And many virgin girls love to show-off their pure little bodies running around playing and frolicking on the sand and shore, finding every little reason to laugh, yell and scream; all the while knowing very well how they're capturing attention and temptingly teasing the guys.

And last but not least, they can be found at family social gatherings. Mainly because many virgins are quite the homely type, but very family-oriented. Therefore they seek activities (outdoors and indoors) centered around family members and close friends. So, the next time someone you know tells you they're attending a family get-together or someone else's family outing, ask if you can attend.

'Cause, guys, every one knows there's nothin' like a virgin. And most men would do anything to get one. Men know that the man that takes a woman's virginity will always have sexual access to that woman. Because to her, it was her first taste of penile penetration. Even if he had a little dick. And even though his penis was little, to her it wasn't. It probably hurt her... and it probably hurt soooo good! And that very day will more than likely be one she'll remember for the rest of her life... So it follows, that particular man will always own a special place in her heart.

64. Try An Asian Woman.

This suggestion could be a nice alternative for the man with a smaller penis. We could say "*yes*" to this not just on the beauty of Asian women, but on the general stereotype and their physical characteristics alone... that is, physical characteristics of the men and the women. I think it would be okay to say that, more often than not, Asian women are a smaller woman as compared to the height and weight proportion of Black and European women. These two women come in all sizes, but often complain that they are too big. While on the other hand, Asian women tend to favor the profile of being short, small and petite. This might translate to a smaller pussy!

But if that doesn't equal enough common sense to you, let's take a look at their men... forget about their obvious smaller stature; let's delight ourselves in the cruel stereotype that Asian men have *little tiny rice dicks*. Well, maybe not that tiny. But many Asian men do have little dicks. Don't believe me? Then go to a gym where Asian men hang out. You'll see the truth either through the clothes they wear, or the men's locker room. Just think, if Asian men have little penises, then their women must have little tight pussies. I know that's gotta make sense! Because a vagina is only gonna stretch big enough to accommodate what's going into it.

The good thing about that is, to stretch a vagina wider than it usually is could take a long, long time... even with many attempts on a daily basis. This could be very ego-rewarding to a man with a small-penis complex. Just think, the woman would be moaning, groaning, screaming, yelling, pleading, or even crying – out of pain, pure pleasure or both! And if it is both, guaranteed she will never want you to stop... Well, only for a few minutes. But if she is yelling, screaming or crying, ask her if she wants you to take it out. Most likely she'll say *"No!"...* ha ha! What a beautiful thing, huh?

And during sex she's always gonna be talkin' 'bout how big your dick is, and how good it feels inside her. I warn you, though, never let a good pussy like that get away! 'Cause you know chances are, she'll get introduced to a bigger dick than yours. If that happens, no more moanin' & groanin' for you, pal... that'll be for her new beau. And word to the wise; they got some Asian men out there pretty much *packin'*, as well as average. So don't be getting all happy from some general stereotypes like you ain't gonna run into an Asian girl throwin' that ass back at you! But chances could be slim. Just proceed with caution. Let's stay to the objective and delight in their generalities and stereotypes shall we... because this could be a good thing.

So, if none of this still isn't convincing enough, then take a good look around you, and see this prevalence of all these other races with Asian women all of a sudden... And just 'why' do you think this is? Because of the stereotype that Asian woman are submissive? Yeah right, dickhead!

65. Fight Fire With Fire: Find A Woman Who's Insecure About Her Breast Size.

Okay, so you have a small-penis complex and often stress about your past sexual performances, and a negative sexual comment a woman may have given you about your penis size in the past. But in no way think that you're alone, because there are a mass of people in this world who by nature are the emotionally weaker, and tend to be more emotionally unstable about their psycho-biology to a degree at least double: they are called *women*.

Sexually, while men are uncomfortable with their penis size, women are most uncomfortable about the size and shape of their breasts. This most private and personal insecurity has left women so emotionally distraught that very often they feel extremely troubled, mentally confused and sexually distracted. But unlike most penis-insecure men, breast-insecure women are driven more madly by the problem. Even to the point where many go a step beyond in an attempt to remedy or compensate by seeking a plastic surgeon for breast augmentation or breast implants.

So fellahs, if you ever get a woman that fits this category, or better yet, get a woman who asks you, *"Do you think my breast size is okay?"* – keep her! For she is a precious gem! 'Cause chances are, if she revealed her emotional insecurities enough to ask an intimate question like this, she's really diggin' you, boy! She likes you so much, that she feels comfortable around you. But this same question has a deeper meaning... sorta two-fold:

1. She wants you to know she accepts you for who you are, with all your physical attributes, as imperfect you may think they are.

2. She immediately needs to know if you accept her for who she is, along with all *her* physical attributes, as imperfect as she thinks they are.

Chances are, she wants the relationship to be permanent, but first, needs some extra-thick reassurance.

66. Develop A Fetish For Overweight Women.

Okay, let's weigh the pros and cons (pun intended). What woman (especially in America, where thin is always in) is most caring, most understanding, most sweet, most sincere, most considerate, most thoughtful, most dedicated, most loyal, most respectful, most loveable, most worthy of love, most receptive to love, yet most unloved? The woman who's over weight, of course – the fat woman. But you knew that already, right?

Here's something else you probably already knew: fat women have the best personalities. And they usually have pretty faces, too, huh. And man, can they sing! What is it with fat women and singing? They didn't come out with the phrase *"It ain't over til the fat lady sings"* for nothing. But your question: *'Where do I fit in this relation, and just how does being with an overweight woman address my particular need?'*

Well, fat women usually possess another quality that's extremely important to your insecurity: empathy. Overweight women are known to be very empathetic towards other's problems and insecurities. Mainly because of how society views and treats overweight women. They are often looked at with scorn and disgust. And are treated with disrespect and neglect by many. But what probably hurts overweight women the most, is their affairs with the opposite sex. They are the most picked on and overlooked of all women in regard to intimate and sexual relationships, even by equally fat and overweight men. Totally unattractive men are quick to skip over 'em too. The nerve, huh? Especially 'cause the fat woman will make just about anybody feel beautiful and good enough, even the little dick guy.

This guy never feels he's good enough. Often solely on account of his small penis. But with the overweight woman's kind nature, understanding and empathetic heart, she is able to sincerely give him loving and caring words, uplift his dampened spirits and work on strengthening his weakened manhood. One thing about a fat woman, although she probably desires a quote-unquote *'normal'* guy, she too would love to have an intimate relationship with a man who believes he has a mental/ physical insecurity that's making his life miserable. In this way she hopes to sort of 'equal the playing field', so they can each lessen the others' emotional hardships and began to focus on each others' good qualities.

The good thing for penis-insecure men is that this is almost never a *one-month* thing, or an *only lasting for the first part of the relationship* kinda thing. This is virtually continuous behavior by overweight women. It seems that they were gifted with a kind nature and soft heart that complements others, bring out the best in others, and they sustain this thoughtful nature throughout life.

We especially see evidence of this when a once-large woman loses weight or becomes thin. Although the weight loss might go to their head they always appear to be foremost against mentally abusive relationships and cruel and hurtful words aimed at people in general. So just think, men, even if she loses some weight to where she feels she's more attractive, odds are great she'll remain with you.... The Creator's kind gift, huh?

67. Don't Be Promiscuous In An Attempt To Find The "Perfect Fit".

One of the biggest mistakes of a man who believes his penis size is inadequate, is to become promiscuous in an attempt to find that *perfect fit*. Guys, I know this penis insecurity issue is already difficult enough to deal with as it is. And it is causing much misery in your life. But having sex with woman after woman, hoping to find that hand-in-glove type fit are odds just above finding a needle in a haystack. Believe this! And even though it may be fun, it is also very frustrating. Being promiscuous will only lead you full-speed ahead to a life less fulfilling, no woman in your corner, no woman to call your own, and a very bad, humiliating reputation. The latter, of course, you don't want. And how could you not end up with a bad reputation? C'mon... you're angry because the women you're having sex with don't give you any signs, clues, body or facial expressions indicating that they *feel* you, that they are being satisfied by you, or that they're experiencing pleasurable pain. Or maybe just because you aren't getting any call backs... Which one is it? All of the above?

And if you're angry because of this, chances are, she is too. And you know how women get, even when they feel a man didn't treat them right in bed... they run their mouths... to other women... Ones they do know and ones they don't know. And you know it ain't nothin' like a woman who felt cheated in bed. Especially if you just met her. Because she's gonna tell it all. Right down to the very last half-inch! Yeah, pun intended... You're gonna get it, pal. Because when it comes to sex, some women cannot stand a man with a little dick.

So tell me, what kind of reputation with the ladies could be worse? Get this kind of rep started and you won't only lose 'face', but something far more valuable... an inch! So, really, what you want to do is concentrate on just finding a woman whom you like, and one whom you feel truly likes you. A woman who seems to accept you just the way you are. Even a woman who tells you, *"I love you and there's nothing I would change about you"* – even if you think she's lying. Maybe she is... but in that very statement she also expressed that she's willing to overlook imperfection in exchange for your commitment to her. Just remember, fellahs, It is *'cheaper to keep her'*... financially, as well as health and reputation-wise.

PART IX:

PENIS-INSECURE MEN NEED LOVE TOO – DATING & RELATIONSHIPS WITH WOMEN

68. Keep Your Breath Fresh, Teeth Cleaned, And Wear Cologne.

There's just somethin' about a man with good hygiene. And a man who smells good! Now, I don't floss as often as I should... Once a month, probably twice, tops. Some dentists say you should floss once a day. Others say, after every meal. Either opinion is too often for me. However, I do remember a woman once complimented me on how clean my teeth were and how odorless my breath smelled. But way before the actual comment while she was talking to me (in a very low voice, mind you), her mouth kept moving close and closer to mine as if she were gonna plant a wet-one right on the kisser! Damn, I thought that woman was gonna stop-up my throat with her tongue. But to my dismay, she hesitated and said, *"I can't believe how clean your teeth are. And I can't even smell your breath!"*

Tripped the hell outta me... not because I thought she was gonna kiss me and then didn't. But because of the compliment on my teeth. Heh, maybe she forgot her glasses, 'cause my teeth are many shades from pearl. Not to mention, the suckers need braces, bad!

But I just humored her and went along with it. And later asked myself, 'What in the hell made her say that?' Then I remembered, 'Oh yeah...I did floss this morning. And brushed the back of my tongue real good with the tooth brush.' I'd never have thought these two things in themselves could provoke a seductive advance from a woman. And ever since then, I upped my flossing to once a week. But the tongue-brushing thing? – every time I brush my teeth!

Listen fellahs, a major turn-off to anybody, regardless of gender, is bad breath. This overrides model-type looks, great sex and social status. If you constantly have bad breath the word will get out with the ultimate quickness! And people will do their best to stay the hell away from you! Fortunately, bad breath can usually be taken care of by brushing the back of the tongue (as far back as possible) with toothpaste or mouth freshener. One more thing that scores high with women on the first impression: a man who smells good! So wear good cologne. I know there's countless times you've heard a woman say, *"I love a man who smells good."*

That's because women do. It makes them just wanna be all up under him! Makes 'em wanna bury their face all in his chest, even if he doesn't have one. Oh, yeah, one more thing never to forget... Always put a dab or two near the crotch area. Sometimes a woman is known to *'follow her nose'...* and even if she finds a penis she thinks is smaller than average, she'll probably ignore it as a turn-off and give you some head, on hygiene points alone. Then chalk it up as, *"Well, it smelled good"*. These three hygienic tips are key to a woman not thinking twice about getting close to you. And it greatly improves intimacy.

69. Try To Say "Yes" To Suggestions For Dates And Appointments With Your Woman.

Whether insecure or very secure about ourselves, many of us at one time or another for a short duration at least, say *"no"* to suggestions for dates and appointments with our women. Reason being; we are just too busy for them, and can't seem to get around to it. Once the sheer excitement of a new relation wears down, we tend to be more settled in the relationship – taking some things for granted and taking everything else less seriously. But by routinely failing to accommodate her invites, you will find other crucial aspects of the relationship suffer, such as relationship-strengthening quality time, one-on-one occasions, and essentially needed sexual relations. All of which complement the other, and are fundamentally necessary to her sense of well-being and stability in the relationship. Women want men to take their sex life with them seriously! And not take them for granted just because men know they can get sex from her just about anytime they want it.

Funny thing is, just about every time you want it, she wants it too. She just wants you to butter the bread before you eat it! She wants to go out on dates, attend dinner meetings, take walks on the beach, and then order good sex for dessert! Problem is, he often just wants to skip right to dessert. And this really displeases her. As a matter of fact, this is one of the fastest ways to make her feel cheap and unappreciated.

Continually neglecting to accompany her on dates and get-togethers sends her clear discouraging messages. She interprets these messages as:

– *"You don't wish be seen in public with me";*

– *"I'm not pretty enough, or worthy of being on your arm in public";*

– *"You will feel embarrassed because of me";*

– *"You don't want other women to see you as already taken";*

– *"You are cheating on me and are afraid of getting caught."*

All these will be among the first thoughts entering her mind when you turn down a date with her. And to make things worse, you still insist on having sex any and every time you want it. Add all this together and you've got one angry and irritable female.

This behavior of yours will be very effective in lowering her sense of her desirability quotient. She will begin to feel like she's 'easy', - easier than a bar-hop-bimbo on a Monday night. Frustrated with the situation, she will immediately assess the only relation she feels you have... a sexual relation. And just how good is that? If she never before tripped on your past poor performances in bed, and the fact that you have a little penis, she's gonna definitely trip now! And you'll be *outta there* like yesterdays paper!

Still too busy? I don't think so. Make time to enjoy intimacy with your mate – wherever she may want. And you'll discover that all those other things you are trying to do or trying to keep away from her are not that important after all. Plan at least one night a week to spend outside of the house – just the two of you. And frequently do little things to let her know how much you care for her, appreciate her and that you love her. And the next time you make an excuse or are too busy, she won't even trip.

70. Condom Shopping In A Grocery Store With A Hottie On A First Date Will Only Allow Her (And Everyone Else In Line) To Know How Small Your Dick Really Is.

Time on a first date should never be spent together with the girl in a supermarket or drugstore. That last minute attempt to grab some alcohol and condoms will always work against you. C'mon, think about it... Any booze you choose is gonna make her think, *"Yeah right, I ain't drinking that Date Rape juice!"* Or at the least, put her on the defensive alert of your intentions to get her drunk, and pressure her to have sex on a first date, especially if she didn't intend to.

But even all that ain't the scary part... The scary part is headin' toward that counter, knowin' you haven't bought condoms yet. Now, of course she's right there with you watching the cashier ring-up the pleasure juice & chips. But unfortunately, that very moment brings out her calculated first date question; *"You gonna get some condoms?"*

Boy oh boy, let me tell you! If you got a little penis and are already feeling nervous, you better be thinking about jumping ship right now! Or you could take the lesser cowardly route by saying you forgot your wallet... Just get the hell outta that line with her.

But if her question only makes you a bit nervous, then *man-up*! Tell that cashier you need some condoms! And watch your hot date, the cashier, and everybody else's nosy ass *turn, in unison,* toward that glass case in the corner...

Cashiers always seem to alarm everyone in the surrounding area with that big ring of keys, and pointing to all the condoms with a classroom yardstick. And of course, the only ones easy-to-get-to, up-front-and-center are the Magnums: Extra Large... Luckily those aren't the only ones in the case. So the cashier continually points around selecting other brands until you give a nod of approval. Funny thing is, during this time the store seems to command absolute silence from everyone. With only to be heard striking taps of the glass with the yardstick, and a dramatic drum-roll in the background.

The cashier seems to delight in the high and low facial expressions by the hot date while pointing between two sizes: too big and too small. And then, immediately after your non-approval of either *Large* or *Extra Large*, the clerk rubs it in with a soft smirk and a light chuckle to follow.

So, which ones you gonna choose, dickhead? Absolutely No Points awarded for *regular* size. To choose those you're damned if you do, and damned if you don't. The embarrassment is all yours this time. Next time, make her wait in the car. Because guys still haven't figured how to smooth out an invasive, indecisive situation like this one.

71. Don't Act Too Childish.

When one has a distinguishing feature (mental, physical, or emotional) that he believes, or society at large believes, is undesirable, undeveloped or just immature, caution should be taken to refrain from anything that is characteristic of that feature – especially if it can bring misery and discomfort.

Likewise, if you're a man whose penis is too small, one of the worst things you could do in the presence of a potential mate is act too childish and immature. But don't get me wrong, this shouldn't be confused with laughter and being humorous. After all, having a great sense of humor is often what attracts a woman to a man in the first place. Plus laughter breaks the ice and helps break down inhibition.

But outright silliness should be avoided. Often being seen acting childish in front of a perspective mate could make an irreversibly negative first impression. It could influence the woman to think he is infirm, immature and acts child-like on a regular basis. These thoughts can cause a woman to question and have doubts about a perspective relationship, leaving her to wonder of her own safety and security with this man, not to mention the stability of the relationship. It's not that a man has to be serious all the time, because life is serious enough; but a woman must have the reassurance that she is dealing with a real mature man, and not an adult male with a child's mentality.

There is a time and a place to let the little boy in you come out. As a matter of fact, a woman loves to see her man phase back to innocence and lose himself in his boyish qualities. But a mature man knows when to put him back in. While she enjoys seeing him running around acting silly with his kids, talking in baby tones to the pets, even playing like a child with her – whether that be hide-and-go-seek, hopscotch, playing house or playing doctor. But at the mere moment a woman wants him to get serious; she can place a hairline between maturity and anything less. At these sensitive but serious moments, if he acts anything less than what is necessary she could become extremely agitated and silently furious, dismissing his manhood.

And of course if a woman goes as far as dismissing your manhood, you can forget all about introducing her to your little penis, or anything else for that matter. A real woman is looking for a real man – not a boy. Even if the woman is attracted to you initially on face value, whether that be a handsome face, a masculine body, nice and tall or whatever, as soon as she gets the slightest hint that you are childish and immature, she's likely to seriously rethink if her shallow attraction is worth all the future problems and headaches you'll put her through.

And for some unknown reason, some women even go as far as equating immature juvenile behavior in a grown man with another child-like characteristic – a little penis to go with it. So, because you already have a little penis, don't act childish.

Instead, accentuate another quality of yours – one that won't wane with time. That way, she'll go into the relationship latched on to that particular quality; and when it's time to introduce her to the *little guy,* she won't think much of it. (No pun intended.)

72. On First Meeting A Woman, Don't Let Her Know How Much It Bothers You.

Men who have profound negative emotions about their psycho-biology usually allow them to manifest themselves during their daily lives. These negative feelings reveal themselves in everything from being less enthusiastic about life, to expressing low self-esteem and constantly showing self-pity and putting oneself down in front of friends. Some of these men feel so troubled about their emotional instabilities that they swear it will be the cause of the destruction of any intimate relationship.

Consequently, they feel it almost impossible to enter into a prospective relationship without first warning the woman of their emotional problems. Even though, by allowing their emotions to run wild, they run the risk of upsetting the very woman they were most anxious to please. And the woman will likely exclude him from being a potential mate indefinitely! Mainly because she sees him as weaker than he should be. She sees him as being less manly – his masculinity somehow being compromised by feminine traits. She also sees a gender role reversal: instead of her finding a firm emotional support for her troubled nature, she finds him projecting his insecurities on her and needing her emotional support along with reassurances.

But because there is somebody for everybody in this world, even the most insecure man bent on wearing his emotions on his sleeve can find someone perfect for him. Everyone knows there are plenty of women who make the point that they would love to have a man who readily shares his inner most personal feelings with them. These women see it as a bonus! A man who will be tender and loving. And a man who-will empathize with her and her sensitive needs.

Then, of course, there are those women who'd prefer to take the aggressive role for themselves, and are attracted to their opposite... the weaker male. But this could backfire, because they could end up despising each other for being opposite. In time, they'd grow to resent the very qualities that attracted them in the first place.

When two mixed emotional opposites meet and connect, each one is projecting some unwanted part of themselves onto the other in an attempt to disown that negative quality - to disclaim it! Each continues this behavior to convince themselves it is not a part of their own make-up. But troubled waters are bound to flow, because soon we dislike that quality in our mates – even though we have admired it at first! So heed the suggestion: *On First Meeting Your Woman, Don't Let Her Know How Much It Bothers You.*

73. Don't Tell A Woman You've Never Sexed That You'll 'Rock Her World'.

One of the major drawbacks of being an undisciplined, sexually unrestrained male with a big ego, is that he often sticks his foot in his mouth, saying things about himself he doesn't even believe; and declaring many others he has serious doubts about. Problem is, while in the routine of promoting his so-called qualities, someone's going to challenge him, demanding a show of proof. In other words, put up or shut up!

Fortunately though, for the most part men with smaller penises aren't very boastful. And even though many have egos just as big, they are less likely to manifest them verbally or walk around wearing them on their sleeves. But at times there are exceptions to the rule... and like men with bigger penises, less endowed men will brag and boast of their sexual prowess, either to prove themselves or just to get laid. Yes, men with smaller penises tend to be quieter and somewhat shy; they harbor physical and emotional insecurities to a fault; and are more apt to have lower self-esteem and sexual-esteem. But none of the above changes the fact that they are still typical males with huge egos and gallons of testosterone to boot, and love pussy just as much as the next man!

With all that said and done, men with small penises must exercise explicit verbal restraint when speaking intimately with a woman whom they've never had a sexual encounter – even in raging-hormone desperate situations. Because when you come clear out of the blue and tell a woman whom you never sexed that you will rock her world (and it's doubtful you could make good on it), you spread yourself too thin. Plus, you run the great risk of her misinterpreting how you meant that statement. She may take it literally or figuratively. (Although highly unlikely), she may take it to mean that you will treat her like a queen, work hard to satisfy her, and please her in all aspects of a relationship.

But odds are she will take it in a general sense because she knows when that particular statement is coming from a man it could *only* mean that he intends to make her feel good like no other man by sexin' her down in bed and driving that pussy to the hilt! Or, that he has this huge dick and plans on pounding her vagina until she continuously screams into her ultimate submission to him.

So, as you see, from a combination of how she perceives you, along with your physical mannerisms with the tone of that statement could make her come running to you with open arms... or flee fright-quick fast and in a hurry! Willing to take that chance? Wouldn't be wise to... 'cause even if she took it that you'll treat her like a queen in all aspects of the relation, who could live up to that? It could be an uncompromising burden, and she'll hold you to it!

But even all this couldn't be all that bad compared to if she took it to mean that you had this huge dick she could ride on like a rocket to the moon. Just think what her reaction would be if you couldn't sell her that ticket?... And the outcome? Major disappointment over your beguiling deception!

And what of your own feelings when the day comes for lovers' showdown at high noon? Well, let's just call it *noon* because there won't be nothin' *'high'* about it! At the very least you could feel totally embarrassed and utterly humiliated.

If the base of a relationship was built on the statement *"I'll rock your world"*, then how could it possibly go on if you can't deliver the goods? I mean, it's not that a woman has to have a big dick and all, but she'll kinda hate you for lying from the get go. And you'll probably never want to see her again in life for making your manhood feel questioned, rejected, and dismissed. So back to the rule: Don't tell a woman whom you never sexed that you'll rock her world – 'cause she could put a rock in yours.

74. If She's Always Having A Good Time With You Before Initial Sex, Don't Bring It Up.

This suggestion is more for the man who is not looking for a temporary or short-lived relationship, but for the man who is more sexually disciplined and less sexually crazed when it comes to the first few dates on meeting a woman; a man who forces himself to undergo patience towards his carnal desires, and instead allows a relationship with the woman to stem from other things such as friendship, mental chemistry, trust and compatibility. This way allows the couple to first receive one another as simply friends and have fun together. To build communication with each other. And to interact on a personal level.

Men need to understand that women want more out of an intimate relationship than just sex. Some women must first know (before any physical and verbal commitment on their part is made) if the relationship has the potential to be a lot of fun for them. Women want to often experience the wonderful things that brought them together in the first place; like sharing and laughing at each others' corny jokes; acting silly and childish with each other; going for walks and exercising together, enjoying concerts, movies, and laughing in stand-up comedy clubs. And just being spontaneous and enjoying life together.

If the woman believes her desired personality characteristics in a man have been met, she will immediately become more intimate with you and shortly after offer her love to you. If at all at this time you feel the need to express your emotions or insecurities by telling her you think your penis may be too small for her, be very careful... this revelation could prove disastrous to a once highly prospective relationship. Your underlying tensions could aggravate the situation. Even if the woman doesn't care about penis size, she may view this revelation as a weakness in your character. If you start communicating your sexual insecurities over and over, be prepared for the worst. If she does stick around, at the least you can expect personality clashes and undue frustration.

Remember, if a woman (before initial sex takes place) decides she wants to settle down with you, it should be looked at that she accepts you for exactly who you are, irregardless of your personal opinions of yourself.

75. If Before Initial Sex A Woman Assumes You Have A Big Penis, Cancel The Date Indefinitely!

One way to quickly end a potential relationship before it even begins is when one person expects much more than the other is able to give. But when a person's physical development is in question, a new relationship with an unforgiving, over-expecting partner will be a fast ticket to emotional misery.

For a man with a woman who thinks his penis is too small, this emotional misery can be magnified. If you're in this kind of relationship already but can't seem to get out, well, good luck with that. But for future reference, spare yourself all that mental anguish by not even bothering yourself with women who are attracted to big dicks.

Slight problem though… how does a man even know if a woman is attracted to big penises in the first place, especially if she never mentions it? Answer: you don't, not really. If the woman is not verbal about it, you have to rely on your other senses to discern.

There's other signals you could pick up on, though. Like her mannerisms in the way she holds, touches or handles phallic-like objects in your presence, especially big phallic-like objects. I mean, if there are a couple of phallic-like objects in the room, yet she picks up the larger one and starts to fondle it suggestively or seductively, then this could be a clear sign. And another time pulls a similar act choosing the bigger object (before initial sex) for the second time in a row, and added some soft sighs and panting, I'd say that's a dead giveaway! She's a big dick lover! – don't chance her. (Better yet, take your little wee-wee out your hand and ditch da bitch!)

But some women are less assertive in their methods of trying to figure out whether or not a man has a big penis. And even more subtle in their mannerisms on letting a man know they prefer larger penises. Women nowadays, like to believe they can tell or judge whether a man has a big penis or not just by the way he walks; the depth of his voice and the way he talks, the clothes he wears, and the way he wears them, whether he's bow-legged, long-legged, short, skinny or tall. Other women like to let a man know that they're partial to bigger penises by interestingly telling him that he has big feet, large hands or a big nose. Even though these are complete myths and stereotypes with absolutely no scientific basis, women swear by them, as do some men.

So if a woman (whom you never sexed before) for no apparent reason takes a sudden interest in the size of your nose or the size of your hands (and even starts playing with your fingers), or reveals to you she has a foot fetish – watch out, pal! Better ditch her quick!

76. Don't Act Too Masculine Or Overly Aggressive With Women.

This suggestion can be taken for all sorts of reasons. Women want and need to feel comfortable with men and around men. But a man's need or inclination to show-off his machismo often times gets in the way of her comfort. A good thing not to do when first trying to get to know a woman is to act like *Me Tarzan, You Jane;* or even worse, like a straight-out caveman from early Europe, when dealing with her. This behavior says to a woman:

"He's way too aggressive for me."

"His aggressiveness is very intimidating, and I'm scared to resist."

"I fear for my safety."

"He could hurt me without even knowing it."

"His aggressiveness would allow him to intentionally harm me. I better keep my distance."

This kind of behavior reflects poorly especially on a man who has a small penis. Reason being, a large penis is thought of as very masculine, and no doubt, potentially highly aggressive during sex. But a man who acts overly masculine and very aggressive, yet has a little penis to go with it, is doing himself a great disservice by acting this way. Because with women those two don't go together. He looks like he is trying to over-compensate, just like the little guy with the oversized muscles.

Matter of fact, women are very quick to make a laughingstock of it among female friends. And when this news of your misfortune gets back to you (and it eventually may, depending on the woman's dislike for you) it will most certainly become one of the worst, or *the* worst dilemma in your entire life. Because this is a direct blow to your manhood. The wound may or may not be everlasting, but definitely has influential power to negatively impact your attitude when dealing with women.

The thing is, when women view or experience this rough aggressive behavior from a man whom they never had sex with, some of them skip right over the potential bodily harm, and parlay it directly to vaginal harm. These women think; *"Oh, he's got a big dick to go with that behavior and he can't wait to try and pound my pussy 'til I cry or 'til I bleed."*

Or, *"He wants me in a sexual position totally at his mercy while I beg him to stop!"*

Fellahs, those types of women are not the problem. But rather, the women who see or experience this macho behavior from you before initial sex takes place. These women connect that attitude with a big dick and aggressive sex. They like, want, expect and anticipate a big dick and aggressive sex, in the equation. And if you don't have the last piece to this puzzle, you've just created a huge problem for yourself!

77. Don't Be Too Flirtatious.

Men, you gotta realize that women aren't dumb, they actually do have brains. We know they can feel emotionally like us, but rarely do men admit (or even understand) that women are the more keen at detecting child and adult behavioral patterns, cross-gender mannerisms, and male and female sexual conduct. To put it in a nutshell, women know more about men and other women than men know about either.

That's why men have to be extremely careful when it comes to flirting with women – especially if they're trying to keep other women from noticing. But their success rate is near zilch, because, when it comes to come-ons, a woman's senses pick-up like radar antennae.

And even though many women fall for it, most of them know that a man who appears to be flirtatious shouldn't be taken too seriously because most of what comes out of his mouth is nothing but a bunch of insincere, empty compliments used to grab her attention.

If the woman gives her attention long enough for him to say things she feels are totally untrue (and that she can't live up to) she will take his flattery as exaggerated, and view him as desperate. Desperate men are also looked at as weak and infirm; men with little pride; and men who sell cheap goods at giveaway prices. And when men sell themselves so cheap, women know they're words are too good to be true, or not worth much.

It seems very odd, but certain sexual gestures and overtures made by women directed at men are taken by men to be major turn-ons and unmistakable sexual invites – such as a women seductively licking an ice cream cone or sucking on a popsicle. But similar acts from men directed at women are not seen so favorably. As a matter of fact, copy a woman in this manner and it could be a fast ticket to rejection.

Don't get me wrong, women like to be flirted with, and even more so love the idea that a man finds them desirable enough to give them extra attention. But for mature-minded women who are looking for more than a one–night stand, the actions of an overly flirtatious man arouse yellow and red flags. They tell the woman to be very careful because he's signaling untrustworthiness, disloyalty and infidelity.

But the irony is, when a woman (even a mature-minded one) wants a one-night stand, suggesting you want the same could be a huge mistake, and an unforgivable first impression. It leads her to think the extended attention and flattery you gave her was really nothing special about her, but ordinary male lust-driven hormones. Although, her total plans for you in the first place was nothing more than to expend her own lusts, she wants to feel special and she'd love to believe you were interested in much more.

Oh yeah, I almost forgot... this book is about having a small penis... and just what does this topic have to do with having a small penis? Well, look at it like this way: This topic suggests you not be flirtatious if your penis is too small because when you are flirtatious with women, many women will take it that you are really sexually confident, sexually virile, and sexually endowed – which it follows of course, her thinking you have a big penis... And if she goes into the relation thinking this way, then you reveal something much less, she could become quietly disappointed... but take her revenge in a more cunning manner... or just break off the relation for feeling deceived.

78. Don't Kiss & Tell.

For eons, a woman's pet peeve about giving into a man intimately was the great potential for the man to kiss and tell. But when the man changed that potential to reality, it made the woman even more sexually inhibited. And with the threat of being labeled *'slut'*, *'loose'*, or a *'nympho'*, her thought became skeptical, her sexual passion became fear, and she was less inclined to express her emotion verbally or physically. This unwritten rule of *'don't kiss & tell'* is looked upon as a given – no explanation needed. For many men, honoring it is extremely difficult. But its violation can cause severe tidal waves in calm waters.

But on the flipside, when it's the woman who lets the cat out of the bag, the results can be two-fold – either being a super boost to his ego, or a devastating blow to his manhood. As you know, the latter, is what often happens to the man with small penis-insecurity. To him, he owns a physical undesirability that he never volunteered to buy. It is a painful, fragile secret. To him, she has discovered him, uncovered him, and exposed him. And if that woman is in his social life, there's nothing in the world he wouldn't give to silence her speech. He would be very careful to steer clear of people she talked to, friends whom they both associate with, and any others who might be aware of their intimacy.

But one thing that would help counter these feelings is if the guy has an attractive social personality or a healthy sense of self-worth. 'Cause if she spills the beans (and it should be assumed that she most definitely will) the guy with penis insecurity will need some good character to fall back on.

Guys must remember, *'what's good for the goose is not always good for the gander'*. Guys love to talk about their sexual conquests, but on the other hand hate it if the woman talks about how they failed to conquer them... If you're lucky you'll find a woman who respects your privacy as much you respect hers, if you both remember not to *'kiss & tell'*.

79. *Be More Romantic.*

If there is one thing women request from men over and over, yet hardly ever get, it's romance! It was in the past, is now, and appears will always be in the future the most sought after and yearned for experience women desire from a man. And it is *not*, never was, and never will be a big penis! The average woman would rather have a man with a small penis who's big on romance, than a man with a large penis who neglects romance. Women want to be treated with love, respect, and fairness – not as male fantasy sex toys completely devoid of true feeling and emotion.

Women are by no means asking men to master the art of romance, yet would happily settle for a little extra attention. Women want their mates to be creative and find interesting ways to show her that you care. This demonstrates that you are considerate, sensitive, and attentive, without taking her for granted and just prompting her for sex. For romance is the ultimate expression of intimacy! And reassures her that she's desirable, and appreciated. Women are so starved for romance that it doesn't take much of it to satisfy her. Neither does it have to be expensive – as long as he doesn't spare any expense, of course.

It is very impressive when her man surprises her by delivering a home-cooked meal to her job for lunch. Or sends her a singing telegram. And never forget to mail a greeting card to her work on special occasions. To be more personal, handwrite a love letter to her, or a sweet poem you yourself composed and deliver it to her wherever she may be. Just in case you're not the creative type, surprise her with flowers and a card for no particular reason. And all women love stuffed animals – especially if you won it just for her!

Even if you're low on cash, never let money be the excuse for neglecting romance. Simple romance goes a long way; it is very dear to a woman, and is most unforgettable. Grab a nice tablecloth, sleek wine glasses and a pair of tall candles to put on a table for two, turning an ordinary dinner into something special. Moonlight strolls in the park as well as barefoot sunset walks on the beach are always memorable, and very intimate. Leave *'I Love You'* notes, *'I Miss You'* notes, or notes that say, *'I Thought About You Today'* all around the house where she can easily find them. Call her when she's away just to say something special... make it short and sweet, or even quite silly! Any of these suggestions are everyday simple romance, but are uncommon and thoughtful enough to be a prelude to a night of sexual pleasure!

So here you have it! A quality adjustment every man could use to easily become the romantic partner of her dreams. All you need for sexual acceptance and relationship satisfaction. Sexual attachment doesn't come from a big dick with an arrogant attitude behind it. Deep sexual attachment and all-around satisfaction comes from romance and passion – and a passion for romance.

80. Become More Affectionate.

Although it won't do anything for the size of your penis, being more affectionate with your woman will definitely do wonders for your love life. This treatment is yet another thing women so yearn and desire from their lover, but at the same time dare never to ask for. And if a woman feels that her man isn't giving her enough affection, it usually results in sudden mood swings, unexplained temper-tantrums, and sometimes a bitchy attitude directed towards her man.

Problem is, there are still a lot of areas where men are pretty much in the dark when it comes to understanding what makes a woman tick. And believe me, this one's a biggie! Women want to be romanced, and they want the intimacy, closeness, warmth and caring affection that go with it. Women love to touch their man, and by nature are very affectionate creatures. But just as much or even more so, they enjoy being touched, and being touched all over their bodies.

A woman wants a man to reveal his tender side, and sometimes initiate affection. She doesn't feel comfortable with competing or indirectly begging for his affections time and again. The man who initiates affection has got a woman for life! And because deep down she knows most men are not like that, she will never consider another lover, regardless of whether she thinks he has a little penis.

Often times, a woman wants a man to be affectionate without rushing into sexual intercourse. It means a lot to just sit with her and talk lovingly while holding hands or gently stroking her body. Or sometime during the day simply ask for a hug when she least expects it. She'll love it! It makes her feel wanted. And she'll think it's so sweet.

If she ever comes home and tells you she's had a rough day at work, immediately prepare her a bubble bath and bathe her, saying kind words and gently massaging her body in the hot water. After that, take her to the bedroom and sit totally nude on the bed with your arms and legs wrapped around her and your chest pressed nicely against her back as if you share a skin. Passionately entangled, softly kiss the sides of her neck and around her shoulders, all the while allowing her to feel the slow subtle patters of your human heart.

As all this rare physical affection soothes her body and soul, she'll love you all the more – and never forget you for it!

81. Make The Woman Feel She Matters In Your Relationship.

Many men with smaller penises tend to view themselves with less masculinity, and for this reason behave less assertive in taking the reins of control in the beginning of new relationships with women. This sense of lost control makes the man feel like he matters less in the relationship. Strange thing is, it appears the only way for him to regain his confidence and position is if the woman gives it to him. She doesn't actually have it. Nevertheless, he won't claim it unless she makes an attempt to give it to him.

But one way to get her to make that attempt is to build her confidence, and honor her with an equitable position. This can easily be done by making the woman feel she matters in your relationship. Many women complain that their men just straight-out don't respect their opinion. They complain that their men act like they don't even have a brain, and are incapable of being rational. Women scoff at these trumped-up charges!

They just want to be treated as equals. But that's not to say women want to be treated equal to a man, or treated like a man. That is to say that women want to be treated with fairness in accords to their respective gender. Women want to be allowed to get into their position and fit in it! And this feminine position entitles them to certain rights – including an unchallenged opinion... sometimes...

It must also be remembered that even when you and her disagree – even if you think your woman's comment is absolutely absurd, stupid, or totally irrelevant, make sure your response communicates the love and respect you hold for her. But if your response doesn't, or you are just tired of holding back your true feelings, then be careful not to put her down. Don't belittle her – just shine it on.

Constantly putting down your woman will convey a direct message of your lack of respect for her. In turn, she will become withdrawn. And during communication with you she will be discouraged to speak out or voice an opinion – even in the face of your wrong. So even if you don't need it, seek her opinion. And seek her assistance in matters that concern you both. She'll love you for being understanding and considerate. And most of all for making her feel she matters in your relationship. She'll be so elated over her much-awaited status, that your having a little penis will never enter her mind!

82. Make A Woman Feel Feminine And There's Nothing She Won't Do For You.

If you want a women to fall head over heels in love with you, regardless of any mental, physical or emotional problem you may have, all you have to do is make her feel the way most men don't... make her feel feminine! Many men waste endless time brainstorming, trying to figure out just what they can do to make their women love them more – or at least to the degree she did when they first met each other. That's just it, when they first met each other...

Chances are, you were turned on and wanted very much to impress her. Therefore, you were a total gentleman and placed chivalry above everything else. When a man is chivalrous towards a woman, he demonstrates his most gentlemanly qualities. And just as long ago, chivalry is as much *en vogue* and still appreciated by women.

A woman loves a man who acknowledges her gender by making her feel womanly, and bringing out the femininity within her. And when she finds a man capable of such, and who proves time and again that he's consistent with it, she will adore him, never leave him, and always desire him. And she will never consider something as frivolous and trivial as her man having a small penis as being the cause for tearing apart that great union.

But for some women, being in a relationship with a man who is not chivalrous creates problems. Reason being, she feels deprived of being placed in her rightful position as a woman; she feels he doesn't hold her in high regard; she feels he thinks she isn't worth being treated special, and dismisses her femininity. Women want their man to be a gentleman at all times, and truly believes he should naturally show courteous qualities towards her. Some of the best and most memorable chivalry is free – any man could do it, and it takes little or no effort, yet has huge impact on a woman's sense of honor and security in a relationship.

Chivalrous acts for men are often as simple as opening doors for a lady, offering to take a lady's coat off, pulling a lady's chair out at a restaurant, and at home. His gentlemanly qualities also shine when he is helpful, courteous and brave by sticking up for her when she gets into a sticky situation and can't quite defend herself. But even in this situation, the chivalrous man's distinction is that he never assumes that a woman needs his help when she doesn't, and by his help never intends to place a woman in an inferior position.

Even little everyday gestures have the potential to make a woman feel very sexy, much desired and very feminine... Little things like keeping your word by calling her when you say you're going to call, and showing up when you tell her you're going to show up. Simple intimate gestures are always a plus. If only you knew the magnitude of expressing to your woman in an intimate way that she's pretty... Tell her. She'll feel so feminine. They like to feel that they're pretty – especially from their love interest. Women like men to take time to flatter them, to compliment them on their beauty and their good qualities, to show admiration for their womanly duties, and to expressively let them know when they do something that pleases. Show her in various ways, obvious and subtle, that you thought of her and that you're always thinking of her. That she is adorable, a delicate prize, a jewel to relish, a woman worthy of your love.

So arouse her femininity with your gentlemanly behavior and prove to her that chivalry is not dead. It's just a distinction of class that few men possess.

83. If And When A Woman Dumps You, Don't Be Too Quick To Attribute It To Having A Small Penis.

Getting rejected or getting dumped by a woman is something every man has had to or will have to face at one time or another in their lives. Good thing about it, rejection's been going on since the beginning of time and it doesn't discriminate. Men from all walks, professions, physical abilities, and appearances are slapped in the face with getting dumped. And it hurts us all the same. Rich men, pretty-boy types, and men who are well-endowed feel more shamed and agitated because they are not used to getting dumped. They feel they have everything a woman could possibly want and desire.

But on the other hand, men who are very insecure because they have a small penis are agitated and suffer to an even greater degree when they get dumped by a woman. Every negative event that happens in their personal intimate relations they attribute to having a small penis. These are the kind of men who swear by everything that if only they had a bigger dick, their women would love them more, respect them more, and do anything for them. And that they would be making love to them so deeply that the last thing in the world she'd ever want to do is break off their relationship. This last statement is probably true. But realistically speaking, chances are, what you do and don't do in bed will not be the cause or the only cause for a woman to give you the boot. And having a little penis really wouldn't be considered a factor. Thank God, women don't think like men... they base a man's worth on far more than just having a large penis, or being able to rock her world in bed. Women base a man's worth largely on the other qualities he has out of bed, and how she feels when she's with him.

Women have been known to dump a man for many reasons. But it is the more common charges that seem to surface more than not – like infidelity, lack of communication and lack of commitment. Yes, the big 'C' word has been a huge prerequisite for many women in the last decade. So much so that no matter how much a man can offer her in a relationship, if commitment is not there – better yet, if he doesn't literally make a pledge or promise to her of his long-term dedication, she will look at him as a definite no-go! A woman wants clear and open communication with her man, and will also put an end to a relationship if she is constantly catching him in lies about where he's been or who he's been with. If a woman finds she can't believe anything you say, you're in trouble!

She'll also contemplate leaving you if she feels you aren't sensitive enough to her emotional needs, or if she feels you often downplay her femininity. Make a woman feel less feminine and you just bought a first class ticket to *'outta here'*!

Another sure fire kick-out is for being too domineering and overbearing on a woman; making her feel timid, not taking anything she says seriously, not allowing her to express herself or her emotions, and taking advantage of her sexually.

These are the usual causes for getting dumped, NOT having a little penis.

84. It's Not Just a Penis That Enters Her Vagina, But The Feelings Of Warmth And Intimacy That Can Only Come From Contact With A Masculine Body.

One of the major mental setbacks for men who suffer form a small-penis complex is the simple fact that they put too much emphasis on the penis and its size. Unlike many men who are 90% percent visual and view women as a pair of big breasts, women on the other hand, are just not geared that way. They don't look at a man as just a penis... not physically and not sexually. Even though it is the penis that physically enters the woman's sexual organ, it is by no means the sole or dominant pleasure-giver.

To understand this, one must understand that the nature of a woman's inner being, the essence of her sensuality and sexuality is founded and deeply rooted in emotion. This makes her quite sensitive and stimulated by a man's masculine touch, and his seductive flattering, yet comforting words. And a penis (big or small) in and of itself can in no way give her these added essentials, which are *crucial* to a woman's overall sexual satisfaction. If a big penis alone could provide all of this, most men in the world would be out of a job. Instead, women would go out and purchase huge unrestrained battery-operated thrusting dildos to do the honors.

But to look at the fact that we men are *'still in business'* and even in great demand should tell us that a woman's sexuality requires much more than an unemotionally energized, mechanically sustained apparatus! Penile penetration into a vagina is just one role in an all-star cast, Broadway performance. Other roles are equally important and are ever-pleasurable during love-play; they add the icing to the cake... and yet are all independent of the penis itself.

Intimate roles like wet kissing and slow licking all about her body. Gently and softly pressing your lips against her skin is not only satisfying to the touch but is even more so pleasing to her mind because she knows when one continually kisses another's body that person is so moved and so desires that other person. Emotional roles that add to the variance of touch, like tight, skin clinging hugs that embrace with emotional warmth, while blowing come-hither words across her ears; body stroking, lovingly cuddling and snuggling, and gentle genital caressing to heighten the moment and make her feel feminine, worthy and desired.

Men who carry a little-penis complex and continually harbor a low sexual esteem must internalize the fact that it's not just a penis that enters her vagina, but other feelings of intimacy that positively affect her sexuality, and play a major role to priming her to maximum climax – physically, mentally and emotionally.

Women place various intimacies high on their priority list because these intimacies require touching and feeling and bodily closeness, which enraptures her soul and envelops her body. A man who penetrates a woman with a big penis alone and often neglects intimacy, or a woman with a huge dildo in hand totally absent of intimacy can by no means compare, equate or surpass a man with a smaller penis that comforts and delights her with consistent intimacies.

Some women are even known to have recurring orgasmic feelings simply from intimacies of skin on skin closeness, from touching and caressing alone.

One other thing that drives women wild during love play and the sex act is the man's spontaneous, impulsive behavior – unpredictable fondling, kissing and stroking, quickly gets the woman all stirred-up, raising her blood pressure and making her heart go pitter-patter. This she enjoys because it allows her to have a chance at reaching peak satisfaction... something most women don't often do. And she wouldn't trade that feeling for the world... not even for a bigger penis.

85. Communicate With Your Mate Your Sexual Hang-ups, Likes and Dislikes.

By far the biggest complaint most women have about their intimate relationships is the lack of communication. From early on women rant and rave to each other, with enthusiasm, frustration and anger, about their men not communicating with them. They complain that men don't want to talk in detail about situations and problems that affect him, her or both of them. And it greatly upsets a woman if her man seldom opens up to her, or is totally unwilling to open up and share his true emotional feelings about his life and their relationship.

Communication... why does it really matter? And what role does it play in an intimate relationship? Well let's just say that poor communication or total lack of it, is the underlying root cause of divorce and failure for most intimate relationships across the board – period. Many men with a little-penis complex are usually the quiet type, and in many cases they become introverted, in which their attitude and interest withdraws within themselves instead of focusing on external activities and other people. Consequently, poor, little or no communication takes place in their intimate relationships also. These men are scared to ask their women about their penis size and virtually afraid to open up sincerely about their sexuality.

Reason being, these men (and men in general) place all their value to a woman in below-the-waist activity and their penis size. And when it comes to talking with the opposite sex, they pretty much keep quiet on the issue for fear of becoming exposed, and drawing intriguing attention to something that may or may not be and issue for her, but at the very least, expose his fragile emotions.

These men see their smaller-than-average penises as a real problem, and a physical deformity, yet refuse to look at the many men with true deformities – amputated limbs or illnesses leaving them in wheelchairs – many of whom have nice-looking women. And usually it's not by chance or because these women feel sorry for them. Perhaps humbled by their infirmities, these men provide the open line of communication lacking with most men, and kept them interested by communicating freely about every aspect of both their lives.

Keeping a line of good communication between lovers or potential lovers is as essential to good sex, as any other general quality in an intimate relation. Problem is, men either don't know how to communicate when it comes to expressing themselves to women, or they feel very uncomfortable doing it when it's about their own sexuality.

Some men feel foolish and awkward about discussing with their mates their likes and dislikes about making love. And they're even more embarrassed to have to ask a woman what exactly he should do in order to please her sexually, because he assumes she thinks he is macho, has had multiple partners and therefore is more experienced than she. This macho image men carry around, coupled with foolish guessing and immature assuming is the reason why most men don't have a clue when it comes to 'what turns a woman on'.

Men nowadays must do away with the notorious tradition of being non-verbal when it comes to expressing themselves to women. You gotta stop believing that talking to your lover about sex spoils the spontaneity and ruins the moment, 'cause women aren't buying it anymore. In the past, women have been known to silently endure a man's reticence and accept it. Now they do it reluctantly, and more and more are starting to speak out against it to their lovers. Women are no longer willing to go on months, even years in a relationship allowing the man to persist in performing some sex act (like finger-banging or pulling hard on her nipples) that he swears turns her on, but really feels uncomfortable or annoys the hell outta her!

Likewise, you should be up front with your sexual insecurities and what displeases you. But just so you don't come off as criticizing and judging, or as assuming she's not sensitive enough to your needs, don't bring it up during sex or even shortly after, because at that time emotions are still in the air. But when you find the right time, take your time, but be brief and clear as possible. Remember... women love men who can communicate as well as demonstrate to women their feelings. A woman wants to know what her lover thinks about her, how she makes him feel, and what he needs. And women need his actions to show it. But she also needs to hear it. She wants to hear that she is the only woman he thinks about and fantasizes about when he feels sexy and in the mood. One more thing – she loves it when you talk dirty... but only when she's in the mood, so don't push it if it's not the appropriate time.

86. Indulge In Much Pillow Talk After Sex.

An excellent way to help make up for an average or a poor sexual performance with your woman is to indulge in much 'pillow talk' after sex. C'mon fellahs, you know what pillow talk is, don't you? It's that loving, caring, intimate, unguarded conversation, between a man and a woman while lying in bed. It's that peculiar window of opportunity for you to make love to her feminine mind that only seems to present itself shortly after sex. It's that rare quality-time that most men don't give, and few women receive, though they yearn for it. It's a chance for men to take intimate advantage of her state of heightened emotional vulnerability. And a time when she's most receptive to his commitment strengthening input.

But because most men don't have a clue, they often miss this rewarding opportunity. But if it's so rewarding, why don't most men know about it? The answer's easy... simply 'cause '*women don't tell them*'. Men must understand that women are fickle and mysterious creatures. They don't let on about much of anything yet expect you to know everything. Some women actually expect you to be a mind reader, and will count you out as 'Mr. Right' if you continually neglect her ever-increasing expectations! Others, after encountering a *wham-bam-thank-you-ma'am*, would allow the man to up-and-step and be miserable about the situation, rather than expose herself by asking him or telling him to stay and engage her in soft conversation. Gentlemen, even though she will never tell you, to a woman pillow talk is essential. It makes her feel all goo-goo-lly inside. And reassures her fragile sense of security. It can't be stressed enough, that women fall in love with what they *hear*. Her biggest climatic sexual organ is through her ears.

That's why, with women, the sex act is a two-part process: one physical, and the other intimately verbal. So, deprive her not of the icing on her cake. Lie there with her for at least an additional thirty minutes. And share together mutual loving and caring thoughts, and moments of deep personal feelings. She'll reward you handsomely. You probably won't recognize her giving it, or that she already gave it. But trust me, she'll give it. Her very nature commands her to!

87. Remember: Sex Is Only About 10% Of A Relationship.

The overwhelming majority of times we hear the phrase, *"Sex is only about 10% of a relationship"*, it's not coming from a man; it's coming from a woman. And many times we hear this statement being made by female sex therapists or female relationship experts on TV, which gives it all the more validity. By the sheer fact there are more women than men voicing and believing this notion should tell us men that women are generally less preoccupied about sex, and place more emphasis on the additional 90% of qualities men contribute to make a relationship work. But don't get me wrong, although only 10%, women are still concerned about good sex – even to the point that the lack of it could quickly send the relationship down the tubes!

Nonetheless, their main focus is on the other governing qualities. Because after the basic needs are met, such as food, shelter, clothing and sex, women are also looking for intellectual stimulation, shared values, romantic love, continued pleasures from arousing affection, high levels of intimacy, economic security, commonality of vision, and moments of deeply shared personal feelings. They desire a man who is confident and self-assured. A man of integrity and morals; one who is about commitment. And communication is always a plus.

These are all top priorities for today's single woman. Every woman has specific individual desires and needs. Women are not necessarily looking for someone to support them. They have their own jobs and paychecks to contribute to the family kitty. They desire men who will be supportive of their careers, their dreams, and their goals. And don't forget strong-minded God-fearing men who are sincere in their spirituality. Who are capable of rearing children, with moral, ethical, religious guidance. And able to care for and comfort a family during hard times and disasters beyond man's control.

So don't dwell on just the sex of it! A true relationship that's intended to last must have much more. Get your focus off your penis... you're gonna have to become more considerate, more attentive, and more disciplined in other areas of your relationship to really make it work.

88. Maintain your Attractive Appearance And Spontaneity.

Everyone knows what first attracts a woman to a man is his attractive appearance, and, a bit later, how he carries himself. When she meets him or even sees him, she is nowhere near thinking how big his penis is. A few might be thinking what he can do to her with it, but not about the size of it. And even if you can't make yourself happy about your penis size, you can always make her happy by maintaining your attractive appearance and keeping some spontaneity in the relationship.

Just because you've managed to get her to sleep with you, say *"I do"*, or better yet have managed to stay in an intimate relationship with her for years, it's by no means an excuse to let your appearance go to the dogs. Don't take her kindness and love for granted. And don't allow your daily duties or your hectic lifestyle to cause you to neglect your attractive appearance – the very thing that moved her about you in the first place.

Many of us men make the huge mistake of getting caught up in the idea of rationalizing: *'it's only my wife'*, etc., or *'she knows who the real me is —I don't have to continue trying to impress her anymore'*. This is the type of thinking that women are very displeased with. But not so much because she's not excited about the new *dull* you, but more so because she knows you expect her to look her best at all times.

Men are notorious for this behavior. Many will first lock-in the woman of their desire by keeping their attractiveness alive and treating the women like a queen for the first few months. Then, soon as the man feels he's got her whipped, he starts slacking in his appearance, getting lazy and turning into a couch potato. Depending on his emotional stronghold over her, he may even go so far as letting his body go to flab, while at the same time never hesitating to express his displeasure when his woman gains weight or loses her hourglass figure that mainly attracted him to her in the first place. Men don't truly realize the mental, physical and emotional pressures they place on women to maintain that sexual attractiveness.

But what these men need to realize is that women are turned off by flab just as much as men are. And women are turned on by a man who makes a constructive effort to please her through maintaining an overall attractive appearance. She likes him to wear physique-flattering clothes and enjoys watching his body wear them. She likes his hair looking neat, breath smelling kissably clean and nails trimmed. In essence, never let her forget how beautiful and handsome you really are.

Also, remember to be more spontaneous in your intimacies – boredom is slow death to anyone's sex life. Skip the same old routine of *'wham-bam-thank-you-ma'am'*, and let the sensual foreplay take on for hours beforehand. See how long you can keep your clothes on, partially taking hers off, while giving her the royal treatment of titillating, teasing erotic pleasures. Watch her try her best not to beg you to enter her – she'll never make it!

Look away from ordinary predictable sex, like the bedroom, and look to more surprising and unexpected places – like your own backyard – or better yet, the tree house! In the kitchen atop of the washer on *spin cycle* is a popular but strange fantasy. And the old stand-by tradition in the backseat of the car is always a winner – and a bit nostalgic, too.

Even a simple but romantic location like in front of your own living room fireplace, while the fire's at its peak, can be a memorable experience. Put the kids to bed early, roast marshmallows together and chat lovingly; then allow the mood to take its course... Even though women love the comforts and privacy of the bed and bedroom, they will never rule out the sheer excitement, spontaneity, and *danger* of getting caught that an odd location provides.

Remember, if you take your physical appearance serious by maintaining self-grooming, she will take your relationship seriously and put in her own personal effort in keeping your sex life alive, and hot 'n' spicy. But don't forget the spontaneity!

89. Find A Woman With Whom You Can Share Your Hopes And Dreams.

I find more than not men with major insecurities about themselves express a profound desire to enter a loving stable relationship that will endure, with the foundation to last forever. Problem is, these ideal unions between couples don't usually occur by happenstance. They have to be worked toward.

The art of finding a woman who you share hopes and dreams with can entail an approach from many different angles. It may involve a life of being in society full-time, socializing with women – friendly, personal and impersonal. It may involve frequently attending outings, conventions and distinctive places that have your specific interests in mind. Or, you may find this special woman by simply interviewing women, asking them straightforwardly and openly about their ambitions, dreams and goals.

There is no one way to achieve this, and many failures and frustrations may arise by way of your methods. In any event, learn from your mistakes, stay to the focus and keep in mind your objective: to find a woman whose top-five desired qualities in a man don't include his penis size, but are rather along the lines of shared dreams, shared goals and compatibility.

90. Find A Woman With Whom You Can Share Activities And Hobbies.

It is very important for a man to feel masculine and manly in an intimate relationship. It is very important for him to feel he's performing great sexually, and it is equally important that he knows his woman is sexually satisfied and is head-over-heels for him.

But for the man who believes his penis is too small to satisfy a woman, he often finds these desired experiences elusive. Consequently, he will try almost anything in an attempt to (at least to some degree) compensate for his sense of loss and inadequacy. For him, pleasing his woman means everything, even before pleasing himself. And her contentment he places first and foremost. Problem is, his focused interest (great sexual performance in bed) is not hers. Her contentment does not revolve around sex and his penis size.

So she becomes dissatisfied and irritated when his actions and communications routinely place sex first and foremost in importance. Although she also loves good sex, her priorities, activities and immediate desires do not directly involve sex – though they can *lead* to great sex. The woman is more concerned with the way a man treats her, the way she feels when she's with him, good communication, and an overall sense of well-being. She desires good social chemistry, too, and the ability to work closely together with her man in activities and hobbies that strengthen their relationship, inspire commitment, and encourage creativity and independence.

She wants you to have a plan, map out specific activities and tasks, give her courage and hope, to support her through them, and see to it that she completes them. Nowadays women have plenty of get-up-and-go about themselves. And they are not interested to just confining themselves to home duties or participating in only girly activities. Women have come a long way and have evolved with great progress. They've become mechanically inclined, extremely competitive, and are no longer afraid to break a nail or get their hands dirty.

Even if your woman doesn't wish to take part in a particular activity you suggest, she'll still feel grateful that you thought enough of her to include her in your doings. And she will take pleasure and get reassurance from the fact that you considered her first instead of one of your male buddies or just doing it on your own.

Spending quality time together on outings, hobbies and other activities away from home builds your friendship and strengthens the bond between you. Women have stressed for years that a close and fun-loving friendship is a vital element for a long-lasting relationship and an enduring, fulfilling marriage. Women place so much emphasis on becoming friends first that many have abstained from sex until they feel a good friendship has been established.

If the man is patient in this way, she will know that he sincerely cares about her feelings and respects her as an individual. And she will adore him for acknowledging her as a human being, with legitimate concerns, needs, interests, dreams and desires that may be totally different from his. A man that does not suffocate his woman in tradition, but supports her independent thinking, cultivates their relation. Just knowing that her input (however minor) really matters to him makes her feel more deeply attached and attracted to him. For she realizes his greatest quality is the fact that he's so unselfish... which is definitely a rarity in men, few and far in between. For this feature, she'll give bonus dividends in the bedroom that'll make you forget all about your *little* secret!

91. Don't Make Too Many Excuses That Your Back Hurts Or You're Too Tired For Sex.

This suggestion is for the man who already has a woman in his life and has probably been with her awhile – even years. He also has a small penis, but unlike other men of less endowment he doesn't stress about it, nor does it make him feel inadequate, insecure, or less manly. His acceptance of himself could stem from many factors: his abilities in other areas more than makes up for his sexual abilities; maybe he uses his small penis well or figures he can satisfy any woman just as good as the man with the larger penis; or maybe he feels secure only because he's still in what he feels is a steady and stable relationship.

A woman, on the other hand, joins a relationship for other reasons, and not mainly for sex. Chances are, she's not in acceptance of herself, often feeling insecure and undesirable if the man doesn't show her constant attention. But if the man starts complaining too much and making too many excuses that his back hurts, or that he's too tired for sex, the woman will soon feel deprived of her due, and even worse, that he doesn't desire her anymore. If he makes the mistake of letting her feel that she's not sexy, she will grow to resent her man.

This will eventually make the union dull and very unstable. What once started out as a relationship built on qualities other than sex will now make or break itself on the issue of sex. The woman will start 'counting her blessings', that is, counting his virtues and counting his faults just to see if it's really worth being in this relationship after all. But since she's an emotional creature, her decision will be based on her emotions, and not intellect or reason. And simply because she feels he is totally responsible for making her feel emotionally unstable and femininely insecure, she will judge him accordingly and start focusing purely on his faults. And if by chance she thinks he wasn't all that great in bed to begin with, plus his penis was a bit on the small side, she will consider it as a major flaw and base her ultimate decision on that.

Remember, all these thoughts will already have been in her mind way before she tells you – if she tells you at all. So if you are complaining to your mate unjustly, then you know what you should do... or, you know what you risk. But if your complaints are sincere about your back hurting or just plain being too tired for sex, I strongly suggest you strengthen your back muscles and exercise regularly to enhance your endurance and improve your overall stamina.

Too busy for exercise? Nonsense! And nobody's getting any younger... except maybe her sex drive! And you're gonna have to be physically fit to keep up with that! If you persist not to, and continue with lame excuses, she'll plot to find some man who will step up to the plate.

So if you're too tired and weary for sex, you must take time to devise a small exercise program. It will be good for your health, and great for your sex life.

92. Don't Lead Her To Think That You Mostly Prefer Bigger Things Or The Bigger Version Of It.

"More is better!"

"Bigger is better!"

Yeah, maybe, in some cases, but don't lead her to believe that everything bigger is better. This subtle brainwashing will soon lead her to transfer that concept to physical anatomy.

In many cases, the small penis in and of itself, is not the problem. Rather it's the man constantly verbally expressing his disappointment with his penis size and molding himself into sexual insecurity. That in itself is usually the problem, or will become the problem. Because women (unlike men) do not like sexually-insecure partners. If the sexually insecure role is going to be played, she'd prefer it be played by herself, and not by the person from whom she needs reassurance. One thing is this: A women is known to take on some of a man's thinking and even more of his ideals. But most of a man's ideals are just that, ideals. They don't manifest, they don't materialize, and not having them doesn't affect his life substantially.

But what does affect a man substantially is what's in his heart. And whatever significant interest is in a person's heart will no doubt manifest itself verbally, over and over again. What is spoken from the heart in words gives off a very unique tone and physical expression to go with it. And when it comes out, a woman's radar immediately informs her to *pay attention* because there is a guy who's getting ready to do something that women have the biggest complaint about a guy not doing – telling a woman what he's thinking, and verbally expressing something that's in his heart. The problem with this particular issue says two things: That it's a major concern, and it's a major insecurity. But the woman in turn views it like: *'Well, I'm glad he thought of me enough to share that with me. But I wish he wouldn't have shared* that *with me.'*

Guys! Do not imprint in your woman's mind that the bigger version of everything is better. Because she will see that you are trying to compensate in some *other* area. Women know that everything a man is concerned about is for a woman's interest, a woman's attention, and a woman's company. She knows a man will try to attain the attributes of another man who appears to have many women – bigger muscles, bigger car, bigger bank account. But if all he has is a bigger penis, and none of these other attributes, men know they can still have as many women as they want. Reason is, because women are the *'Big Mouth of the South'!*

Women absolutely delight in gossiping about their business… and everyone else's business. If a woman gets a taste of a big dick and likes it, she's going to go around town spreading the news to her girlfriends like wildfire! *FREE ADVERTISEMENT* for the man with the big dick. So, when it comes to talking about your circle of friends, keep your mouth in check. Because if you tell her that *'such and such'* has a big penis, (and she probably knows *'such and such'* to have lots of women) then she's gonna want to physically experience a man with a big penis… maybe even *'such and such'*…

93. Have This Attitude: It's Not About You, It's About Me!

A common predicament about having a little penis is that it doesn't just rest with small-penis complex. It can travel through the male psyche and influence other mental states. States like self-esteem, and overall well-being. Also his general status among male and female in social relationships.

With a penis complex, the role of macho status tends to wane, weakening itself and settling in a less dominant position. But in yielding position, a counteraction must also take place. And in this case it usually shows up as the woman assuming more worth and the upper hand in the relation – leaving the man feeling he's lost his edge, his advantage and more important, his respect.

Involuntarily giving a woman control is very dangerous. But getting it back could be even more difficult, because more than likely he has expressed his insecurity to her. Therefore, attitudes change... and she expresses hers as viewing him as lesser. She takes the attitude that, *"I'm the priority in this relation, and what I say goes! And if you challenge me I'll crush your sensitive feelings."* And every so often, just to keep her new-found status afloat, she'll drop subtle but effective *little bombs* on his insecurity.

Now, what he needs to do about *slowly* gaining his respect back – or better yet, avoiding this psychological disaster from jump, the man with the small penis complex should take this attitude, *'It's not about you - it's about Me!'*

I stress this because when a man has an insecurity of such a delicate nature, there is an immediate need to strongly compensate. His manhood must be established right away, and his masculinity made clear to her. This way, even if he decides later on to share with her his most intimate insecurity, she will still give him that basic level of respect worthy of a man. And since he has by nature been given the dominant role, it is extremely important that his priorities come first, that attention be given to his dictates, and his ideas be supported by her. In addition, she must make it clear to him (verbally) that she supports him in what he does, and that he comes first and she second. The latter also needs to be demonstrated by the man – verbally and in action. Even though she might already acknowledge it *('it's about him and not about me')*, she needs to hear it directly from him in order for her mind to confirm it. And every so often, she needs for him to show it!

Now, you might think of this as being a bit cruel, insensitive, and chauvinistic, (and chances are she'll accuse you of all the above), but believe me, she will respect you for it. She'll probably even brag about it to her friends. On the surface, her friends will bash you in reaction. But deep down, they will recognize she's got a man worthy of respect. But beware, 'cause her girlfriends could be after ya... but not to hurt'cha, ha ha. After this, you might still have a small-penis complex. But strong gestures from a man hold more power and influence than a little dick, any day. So hurry up, get the attitude, and show her: *It's not about you, it's about ME!*

94. Don't EVER Go On A Talk Show For Being Guilty Of Infidelity.

Does this really need to be explained? Everyone knows the most popular subject on TV nowadays is secrets and dirty laundry being aired on television talk shows and reality shows. You'd be hard pressed to find anyone in America who's never heard the names Jenny Jones, Ricki Lake, Geraldo, and, oh, I forgot... Jerry Springer!

Probably, the absolute worst thing you could do if you have a little penis is go on a 'trash TV' talk show for being unfaithful. And that's whether you're the guilty one *or* she is! 'Cause when you're on that panel, in front of millions of viewers, you did nothing but jump straight into the frying pan.

And I don't care if you got 99% of the deck stacked against her, 'cause she's got that one *trump card* that'll turn the whole game around on your male psyche! And when she plays it, guaranteed energy and uproar from the crowd! Yelling! Shouting! And laughter... even minutes after she says it.

Major, all-time embarrassment for the man!

And he's gonna be the laughing stock of the entire viewing hour. He's gonna be so at a loss for composure, he's gonna find it uneasy to answer any questions directed at him, or reveal anything against her. He might as well just get up and walk out to avoid any further humiliation thereon. How could he ever get over this? And he'll never forgive her. Is there any worse way a woman can crush a man's masculinity and manhood?

Huh, I don't think so.... A pissed off woman's venom is a bitch, huh? Listen, guys, how many times have you seen a talk show in which the male guest walks on and has absolutely no idea why he's on the show? Countless, right? Anyway, it's always some innocent-looking guy, or one who comes off like he's way too cool coming out on the stage. Sits down, immediately kisses his girl, and then starts grinning at the studio audience. The audience usually starts to laugh because they've already heard the woman's story about his infidelity, (and probably his little dick too). But many times the woman has not yet revealed to the audience about his little dick. Mainly because she knows that's her *'trump card'*, and plans on playing it only when she feels it will command maximum reaction from the crowd, and shock him into ultimate humiliation.

But hold on, guys! Don't be so fast to refuse a once-in-a-life time invitation. She could bring you on just to say, *"You're the best guy in the world... will you marry me?"* Heh heh, fat chance. But earn yourself a chance at an extreme long shot by coming on the show and being very nice to her... Yeah right! – and your odds of winning the lotto are 3-to-1, pal.

So, listen up fellahs, *'who will be the first to volunteer to be a guest on our show?'*... C'mon guys, let's not all jump at once.

PART X:

YOU'RE MORE THAN JUST A SMALL PENIS!

95. Wear A Uniform That Says "Status".

Nowadays, when a woman is out & about on the prowl searching for a man, she hopes to find someone she can identify with; someone whose traits and characteristics best suit her immediate and long-term needs. When she spots a man she's interested in knowing a little better, among the first things she never notices is whether or not he has a big bulge in his crotch or penis contour on the inside of his pants leg.

What most women seek is a man with adult qualities and intangible assets – a man who is responsible and able to provide security. A man who appears to be stable with a sense of direction. A man of status...

And what more says *status* (even if you don't have any *real* status) than a man in uniform? Not only does a uniform symbolize rank and status, it also connotes ambition, power, access and influence, along with everyday essential qualities. Sexually insecure men need to understand that women are not drawn to men because of some imagined sexual aptitude they dreamt-up, nor do we attract women by chance (like they attract us). Rather women act on clues and signals to certain characteristics men give off. Women will find certain characteristics more desirable than others to go hand in hand with her own, plus a few opposites, that still complement her own strengths and bode well for her survival.

Women seek men of status not only from a socio-economic level, but also from an instinctive level. Since women are the weaker in physical strength, it's in their nature to seek security. Wearing a uniform that says 'status' signals strong messages to a female's mating receptors. They in turn cue her to acknowledge some form of power, protection and access to resources.

We all know that women are attracted to men who attract

many other women – and for no apparent reason. But a man wearing a uniform has that same potential, and even more capacity to attract women and for a reason that *is* apparent. A uniform of status generates much attention from women because it exudes power – and women are turned on by powerful men. Even if the man actually has little or no power the woman will (hypothetically) lend it to him – if only just to enable him to win her over and lock her down in a steady relationship. In this case, she is primarily motivated by power, and therefore excuses or never considers his smaller penis. She will gladly make this exception because in most cases a uniform of status conveys the message that here is a man who clearly has his life together, establishes his priorities, sets his goals and is focused on achieving them; a man who is assertive and aggressive; a man who is well-groomed and cares about his appearance.

Status uniforms denote rank, and if it's one thing men who earn ranking uniforms have in common, is ambition. Although ambition is intangible (and its fruits may not materialize for a number of years) it is very appealing, because it signifies future status.

So even if you currently wear a uniform that doesn't rank don't be discouraged, because it's essentially the *driving force* of ambition – which will enable you to move up the ladder – that attracts women. Men willing to struggle to work their way up to gain wealth and resources are held in high regard by women, while men who lack drive and ambition are held in contempt, and their penises are held less too... Probably because they have less women clamoring for their attention – don't you think?

96. Make A Lot Of Money.

Whoever said money couldn't buy them love evidently didn't offer it to the right women! And I'm not talking about call girls. I'm taking about law-abiding, God-fearing, decent women with morals. And good-looking too! These women are to be had by anyone who will have them... But, before you go out scouting there's one important thing to keep in mind: a considerable portion of these women require the man to make a lot of money.

No, you don't have to be a millionaire (though it helps), nor net a six-figure salary. But you must be able to support a wife and three kids comfortably. This easily may also mean keeping the wife up-to-date driving a top- of-the-line luxury sport coupe of her choice, and the ability to take her on a dream vacation every five years. Seems pretty expensive, huh? Well, women are expensive! Just ask any woman her top desired priorities in a man and more often than not she'll rank money among the top five. And most likely, she's not a gold digger. She just wants to be secure and have nice things in life. When a woman ranks money at the top (1st, 2nd, or 3rd), she's clearly saying that money overrules everything and matters most in her relationship. She's driven by it, motivated by it, and will perform exactly to the man's liking as long as she has fair access to it.

And most important to the insecure man is that she feels money transcends all superficialities. She could care less if he's handsome or not. As a matter of fact, she'd probably (due to her own insecurities) rather the man be unattractive or average-looking – to keep down female competition. She also could care less if the man is overweight or not. And the issue of whether or not the man has a small penis is *not* an issue! The thought'll never enter her mind.

But even if the thought did enter her mind, as long as the man could sustain an erection for more than a few minutes, she'll overlook that too. This kind of woman is looking for a man who's ambitious, and has potential. Someone who is confident and self-motivated. She figures if he's not doing well financially, then he must at least have the potential.

Important to her is a high income. But equally important is his willingness and capability to earn a high income. She might be okay with it if he starts off flipping burgers at McDonalds, as long as he aspires to own the McDonalds.

97. Develop A More Intellectual Conversation.

Knowledge... Just how valuable is it? Well, technically speaking, it's the most powerful, useful and invaluable thing known to mankind. And in the hands of the right man, it is the most feared and respected tool a man could possess!

Knowledge and intelligence are so powerful, so influential, and so respected that many maxims and sayings have developed around them. For it was once said, *"Nothing is more honorable than knowledge. The kings rule over the people while the* learned *rule over the kings."*

The validity and truth of this saying can easily be seen in the presidency and his administration: For it is the president's learned advisors and administration that possess the real knowledge and know-how on how to run a government. They supply the president with all the information and instructions needed to carry out the tasks. The president is just the one voted in to represent that information.

A couple more popular sayings are: *"The pen is mightier than the sword"* and *"The ink of the scholar is more holy than the blood of the martyr."*

But you don't have to be a scholar or a martyr in order to have men and women love and respect you. You could take it to a lesser yet still effective degree just by developing a more intellectual conversation. Having knowledge on uncommon and relevant issues along with finding interesting topics to discuss can greatly enhance anybody's life – especially a man with low self-esteem and low self-confidence.

Some men with small penises always manage to overshadow all their own good qualities with a negative perception of their small penis size. Some even believe that it's gonna prevent them from keeping a woman in a sexual relationship with them.

To quickly disprove that belief, all one has to do is turn

within one's own social relations.... There's always one guy who seems to be more informed, and with more intelligent conversation than the rest of the bunch. And because of it, he earns an unspoken prominent position in the group. And although he's usually less attractive, women seem to throw themselves at this type of man!

Reason being… intelligence is very attractive! And it doesn't have a face! – Or a penis for that matter. Intelligence is something you can hear… And remember, women are attracted to what they hear, and not what they see or even necessarily what they feel. Be able to stimulate a woman intellectually as well as emotionally and she won't be able to concentrate on any physical flaw you might have or even that she might perceive. 'Cause her heart and mind will be more preoccupied with that which attracted her to you in the first place – your knowledge and intelligence.

A major factor that can help insecure men come to terms with their small penis is to recognize that most of their relationship problems have more to do with shyness and lack of social skills than their feelings about penis size. Once these men improve on their people skills, it's virtually guaranteed they will become less preoccupied with their penis insecurity.

There's a time for everything – this is the time to feed your mind, your body and your spirit; for only then can you feed and stimulate hers. A good start will be to do more reading; people who are well-read are always more informed. That's why they always have a lot to say, and seem to be more interesting!

Another good initiative would be to attend conferences or workshops that increase skills and knowledge. Because in order to develop new behavior you have to get new knowledge.

98. Strengthen Your Personality.

What can one say about a man with 'personality'? Not much, huh? It's a quality that every person admires in others. And a quality that everyone wishes they possessed. The good thing

about personality is that it makes you shine among others –
even in bad light. And it doesn't matter if you have any
physical, mental or emotional problems, whether real or
imagined. Because personality makes you look good,
interesting, and very attractive to others. To see the truth of
this, just think of someone who has a lot of personality in your
own group of friends, or family members. That someone whose
name is constantly being brought up, whose well-being is often
inquired about, and whose absence is always missed, especially
during dull and boring times.

Whether you think that guy is a jerk or not, or no matter how
unattractive you think he is, there's one thing about him that
you're sure of; the guy's got killer personality! And deep down
you know that's the main reason everyone loves to be around
him. Especially the women.

If a man knows another man has personality, he won't speak
much of it – especially to that guy's face. But because a woman
is so fond of a man with a nice personality, she's gonna be sure
and tell that man to his face. But where she goes wrong about
her feelings is the mistake she makes when telling all her
girlfriends, *"What a great personality this guy has"*. Now all
her girlfriends wanna meet him! Why? Because personality in a
mate is something women always long for.

But unfortunately, most men just don't have *'it'*.

'It' being that personage. That charm and charisma. That
personal identity and individuality. Those habitual patterns and
qualities of behavior that sets them apart from the rest of the
group. And women just plain 'ol admire that in a man. And
they want to be around him all the time. 'Cause personality
livens up everything. Makes bad times good and good times
better. Ask yourself, *'Is there anything in the world admired
more than a unique man?'* Not even an equally unique woman
can compare! And do you think having a smaller penis can dim
that luster? I don't think so!

Heh, even a man with just a little personality goes a long
way. Because his attitude radiates brilliance at certain

moments. Which is usually just enough for the woman to chalk-him-up as having a good personality. Sometimes, all it takes to get a woman to want to be around you is to verbally express interesting (even weird) but thought-provoking ideas. And throw in a little humor to make her laugh every now & then. You'll score huge on humor alone! Women absolutely love a man with a sense of humor. It just keeps breaking the ice for you, over and over.

99. Be A Great Listener.

No! – being a great listener will not do anything to enhance the size of your penis. But being a *'good listener'* is a quality so sought-after by women that, if you have it, it's virtually guaranteed she will forgive any fault you see in yourself – even having a little penis. Early on, beginning from childhood, boys and girls are molded, taught and conditioned by their parents to be a certain way, act a certain way, and to handle problems and situations a certain way. And this learned behavior continues with the child on through adulthood.

Boys are taught to perform. Boys are taught to *act* on a situation or *do* something about a problem. But girls, on the other hand, are taught to *talk* about the problem, to *communicate* about the situation much before actually doing something about it. So, gentlemen, since women generally assert themselves by talking, talking, and talking, we need to listen, listen, and listen. It's very important that we listen (without interrupting) when she shares her feelings, declares her emotions or states her opinions – especially during a verbal altercation. For her comfort and reassurance it is also equally important that we mirror (repeat) what she says just before answering her to show that we've understood. Try to listen attentively to your woman's concerns, whether they are concerns of aspirations, joys or fears. She may not want you to *do* anything except listen – because sometimes all she needs is to be heard and understood. And try hard not to put her down when you disagree with what she says, even if it is ridiculous, sounds stupid, or totally irrelevant to the issues at hand.

If she wants to express to you how her day went, allow her the opportunity – It pleases her… but only as long as you listen.

100. Accentuate Your Greater Assets.

There comes a time in a penis-insecure man's life when he realizes that if he wants to feel better about himself; he must learn to accentuate his greater assets. Some men with smaller penises believe that because of their smaller size they don't have what it takes to keep a woman.

Other men with size insecurity feel that in spite of their size they can still satisfy a woman sexually, but believe that if a woman knows beforehand (and before initial sex) that he has a little penis she will never consider an intimate relationship with him.

Well, in either case, this may or may not be true. But what these men should not do is concentrate their major focus on penis size, or their sexual performance in bed. Rather, they should accentuate and put forth their greater assets.

Reason being, women don't place their major focus on a man's sexual abilities. Instead, women tend to fix and settle their attention on characteristics and qualities the man appears to exudes the most, whether that be negative or positive. Even down to the first few minutes of meeting a guy, many women can discern a dominant, weak, ugly, or beautiful characteristic a man has. In most cases, an attractive quality or asset is what attracts the woman to the man in the first place. And whatever be the nature of that particular quality, the woman will treat him accordingly, even years after the start of the relationship.

For example, if he is a chronic complainer about things he can't change or can change but won't make an effort; or always complains his back hurts and is too tired for sex; or at times emotionally expresses to her that he is not good enough for her

– in bed or otherwise; or just simply comes off to her as being 'weak'; she will always respond (aloud or to herself) unfavorably. And will treat him (openly or covertly) with dishonor, dissatisfaction, displeasure and even disrespect!

At the other extreme, if he always places his best foot forward and accentuates his greater assets, she will likewise treat him accordingly – with honor, satisfaction and respect.

In order to receive a favorable response from women and become more content within yourself, you must change the way you think about yourself and the way you look at yourself. You have to change your focus. Make changes in your life that affect you in a positive way; and make changes in your thoughts that are self-lifting, healthy and productive. Let your good attributes shine!

Everybody has them – and at least one thing they like about themselves. If you're hard-pressed to find one, just reflect on what you believe won over your last woman, or your current woman. Whatever it was, use it again. And if you're still with a woman, then know that keeping her has nothing to do with your penis size! Man does not live on bread alone... and neither does woman!

There must be other things to fill in and around the relationship – to fill in the gaps. Things like personality, chemistry, good communication, compatibility, fun, good sense of humor and spontaneity. Women are also turned on by men who are intelligent, spiritual and somewhat emotional – or at least one who considers her emotions and is sensitive to them.

She's also attracted to honesty, integrity, and of course, fidelity and long-term commitment. And how could a woman not be drawn to a man who's romantic, affectionate and physically fit? Or self-confident, ambitious and self-motivated?

Surely there must be one of these desirable qualities in which you are a master! The man with the little penis complex usually does... If not, and you're already with a woman, then relax, 'cause she's already found one.

101. Keep A Good Sense Of Humor.

Many men who believe they have a physical deficiency, deformity or physical inferiority, usually are men who don't have a good sense of humor as an attribute. Chiefly due to their mental and emotional states they are often less spirited, less lively, and less animated. Consequently, these men can find it very difficult to perceive the funny, the humor and the amusement in happenings of everyday life. Instead, they remain apathetic, unmoved, or feeling and showing little or no emotion.

But this can be corrected by getting out more, mingling with others, and most of all, realizing that lacking this quality, or over-seriousness, is viewed by women as a major downfall! Women rank a man having a good sense of humor so high on their desired priority list that the lack of it would definitely exclude a man as a potential mate. Some women feel that humor is just as important to a relationship as sex. Other women say that since sex is just a small part of their relationship, having a good sense of humor is even more important.

Whatever popular opinion may be, one thing is clear... women want to have fun. Women want fun-loving men who can make them laugh and who can laugh with them. Women want a man who shows flexibility and spontaneity, someone with whom they can relax and be themselves. The most rewarding and fun-loving relationships are not about genitals. The best most fulfilling relationships are those in which couples not only love and lust for each other, but truly like each other and enjoy a close friendship. And in order to have a true friendship you must first establish communication, trust and respect for one another. Then, you will find it much easier to have a good sense of humor.

# # #

www.ingramcontent.com/pod-product-compliance
Lightning Source LLC
Chambersburg PA
CBHW071432090426
42737CB00011B/1640